Your Space

Workbook 1

Martyn Hobbs and Julia Starr Keddle

CAMBRIDGE
UNIVERSITY PRESS

Contents

Alphabet

1 🔊 **02** Complete the alphabet. Then listen and check.

> _b c d ___ f ___ ___ i ___ k ___ m n_
> ___ _p ___ r ___ t ___ v ___ x ___ z_

2 🔊 **03** Listen and complete the names.

1 C _ _ A _ _ L I _E_   4 D _ _ N I _ _ _ _
2 O L _ _ V E _ _   5 E M _ _ L _ _
3 P _ _ P P _ _   6 _ _ O S _ _

Everyday words

3 Reorder the letters to write words.

1 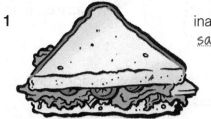   inacsdwh
sandwich

2    VT
....

3    gerurb
....

4    hT-rsti
....

5 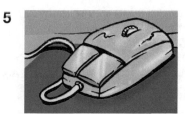   smeou
....

6 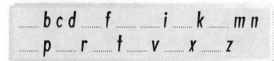   iealm
....

Numbers

4 Find and write ten numbers in words and numbers.

twentyeleveneightfifteenseventhirtytwelvethreethirteenfourteen

1 _twenty / 20_   6 ....
2 ....   7 ....
3 ....   8 ....
4 ....   9 ....
5 ....   10 ....

5 🔊 **04** Listen and complete the telephone numbers.

1 01 ___ 7 86 ___ 224
2 02 5 ___ 421 ___
3 05 ___ 4 66 ___ 01
4 ___ 39 6 ___ 3571

6 🔊 **05** Complete the conversation with these words. Then listen and check.

> It's   old   spell   ~~name~~
> telephone number

Jake   What's your ¹ _name_ ....?
Hilary   Hilary.
Jake   How do you ² .... it?
Hilary   H-I-L-A-R-Y
Jake   How ³ .... are you?
Hilary   I'm twelve.
Jake   What's your ⁴ .... ?
Hilary   ⁵ .... 392 665.

Telling the time

1 **Match the clocks with the times.**

1
a It's half past seven.

2
b It's quarter to eleven.

3
c It's one o'clock.

4
d It's twenty past two.

5
e It's nine o'clock.

6
f It's five to six.

7
g It's ten to ten.

8
h It's twenty-five past six.

9
i It's 12 o'clock.

10
j It's quarter to four.

2 ◦ **06** **Write the times. Then listen and check.**

1 It's _six o'clock._

2 It's _____

3 It's _____

4 It's _____

5 It's _____

6 It's _____

3 ◦ **07** **Match the questions and answers. Then listen and check.**

1 What's the time?
a I'm fine, thanks.

2 What's your phone number?
b He's thirteen.

3 How are you?
c Yes, it's one o'clock.

4 What's your name?
d It's 0135 69348.

5 Is it lunchtime?
e It's five to five.

6 How old is Daniel?
f My name's Olivia.

Classroom

1 Complete the crossword.

2 Colour the flags.

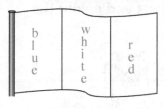

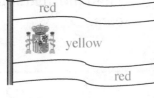

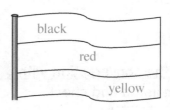

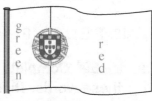

1 France   2 Spain   3 Germany   4 Portugal

3 Draw these things in the school bag.

1 a diary   4 a pencil case
2 a calculator   5 an exercise book
3 two rulers   6 two coloured pencils

4 ⊙ 08 Reorder the words to make classroom sentences. Then listen and check.

1 don't / understand / I / English

....

2 you / speak / can / please / slowly / ?

....

3 you / that / repeat / can / ?

....

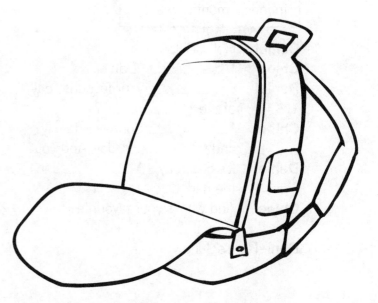

Days and months

1 **Reorder the letters to make the days of the week.**

1 ATRYHSUD _Thursday_
2 IRADYF _____
3 UTDYASE _____
4 YMNDOA _____
5 ENDWASYED _____
6 TDYASUAR _____
7 UDAYSN _____

2 **Complete the months of the year.**

1 J A N U A R Y
2 A ___ G ___ S T
3 A P ___ I ___
4 J ___ N ___
5 O ___ T O B E ___
6 N ___ ___ E M ___ ___ R
7 M A ___ C ___
8 ___ U ___ Y
9 M A ___
10 ___ E B R ___ ___ R Y
11 D ___ C ___ M B E ___
12 S E ___ ___ E ___ B E ___

3 🔘 **09** **Complete the conversation with these words. Then listen and check.**

It's	What's	fun	~~Hi~~
friends	month	week	

Daniel Hello, Chloe.
Chloe ¹ _Hi_ _____ , Daniel.
Daniel ² _____ your favourite day of the ³ _____ ?
Chloe ⁴ _____ Sunday – family and ⁵ _____ day. And you?
Daniel It's Saturday – ⁶ _____ in the park day.
Chloe And what's your favourite ⁷ _____ ?
Daniel It's June.

Ordinal numbers

4 **Complete the sentences.**

1 The f _irst_ _____ day of the week is M _onday_ _____ .

2 The s _____ day of the week is Tu _____ .

3 The t _____ day of the week is We _____ .

4 The f _____ day of the week is Th _____ .

5 The f _____ day of the week is Fr _____ .

6 The s _____ day of the week is Sa _____ .

7 The s _____ day of the week is Su _____ .

5 **Read the instructions and colour the cars.**

1 The white car is third.
2 The yellow car is fifth.
3 The red car is first.
4 The green car is fourth.
5 The brown car is second.

Interests

1 **Use these words to complete the sentences.**

animals   art   books   computers (2)
fashion   films   music (2)   sport

1

My interests are music and computers.

2

My interests are
....

3

My interests are
....

4

My interests are
....

5

My interests are
....

2 **10 Listen and complete the conversation.**

Ben Hello.
Alice Hi.
Ben What's your name?
Alice It's Alice.
Ben How old are you?
Alice I'm ....
Ben When's your birthday?
Alice It's on the .... of

....
Ben Where are you from?
Alice I'm from ....
Ben What are your interests?
Alice My interests are .... and

....
Ben What's your favourite colour?
Alice It's ....
Ben What's your phone number?
Alice It's 0873 ....

Dates

3 **Write the dates.**

1 18/01   The eighteenth of January.
2 10/02   The t....nt.... of Feb....uar.... .
3 12/03   The t....el....th of Ma....c.... .
4 15/06   The fi....te....n....h of ....u....e.
5 13/08   The t....irtee....th of ....ug....st.
6 11/12   The ....lev....n....h of D....ce....be.... .

1 Complete the crossword.

2 Write the nationalities.

1  Spain
She's Spanish ....

3  Brazil
....

2  France
....

4  Greece
....

3 🔘 **11** Complete with the expressions. Then listen and check.

> New York   I'm from   my name's   music   sport

1
Hello! ....
Tiffany.
I'm American.
I'm from ....
My hobbies are
.... and the
internet.

2
Hello, my name's
Deepa.
I'm Indian.
.... Mumbai.
My hobby is
....

4 Look at Dominic's factfile and complete the sentences.

FACTFILE

Name	Dominic
From	the UK
Age	12
Brother	Ross, 14 years old
Mum and dad from	Brazil
Favourite football team	Santos
Favourite thing	my dog

1 My name's ..Dominic.......... .
2 I'm from ....
3 I'm ....
4 My brother .... Ross.
  He's ....
5 My mum and dad are from ....
6 My .... football team is ....
7 My .... thing is ....

be – positive

1 Complete the sentences with *he*, *she*, *it* or *they*.

1  _She_'s Jade.

2  ....'re Sam and Jessica.

3  ....'s Mr Ahmed.

4  ....'s my mobile phone.

5  ....'s Elisa.

6 ....'s a table.

2 Rewrite the sentences. Use short forms.

1 Hi, I am Olivia. _Hi, I'm Olivia._
2 She is British. ....
3 I am in Year 7. ....
4 You are my best friend. ....
5 He is eleven. ....
6 They are in my room. ....
7 We are in Class 7C. ....
8 It is my favourite football team.
....

3 (Circle) the correct form of the verb *be*.

1 I (am)/ is eleven years old.
2 My English teacher **am** / **is** Mrs Taylor.
3 We **is** / **are** in Class 7B.
4 Adam and Max **is** / **are** my friends.
5 Ben **are** / **is** from London.
6 My guitar **is** / **are** in my room.

4 Complete the sentence with *m*, *s* or *re*.

1  She'_s_ from France.

2  They'............ in the school band.

3  We'............ best friends.

4  I'............ from Istanbul, Turkey.

5  He'............ twelve today!

6  It'............ my mobile phone.

5 Complete the email with *m*, *s*, *re*, *is* or *are*.

To: Kate
From: Tanya

Hi,
My name'_s_ Tanya. I'............ American. I'............ from New York.
My mum and dad .... from Russia.
My brother, Boris, ... eight. His favourite football team .... CSKA Moscow. My sister .... 20. She'............ a student.
My best friends .... Lauren and Ellie. They'............ in my class.

Tanya ☺

Regular plurals

6 Look at the picture and write a list.

~~pen~~ ~~book~~ pencil eraser exercise book calculator apple ruler diary mobile phone

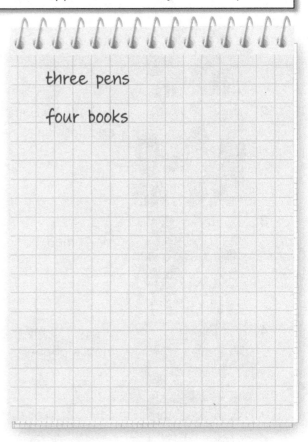

three pens

four books

Possessive adjectives – singular

7 Complete the sentences with the possessive adjective.

1

Hi! .... name's Michael.

2

.... name's Charlie and .... name's Sarah.

3

It's............... exercise book.

4

.... mobile phone is nice. Thanks!

5

Hi! .... name's Lily.

6

.... name is Goldie.

1 **What's in Poppy's bag? Find fourteen things in the word square**

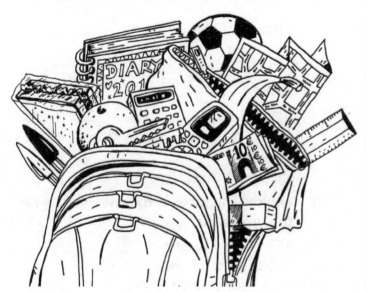

S	R	U	L	E	R	M	B	O	K	O	F
S	B	K	E	S	Z	O	O	K	K	R	O
C	M	G	B	O	P	B	O	B	E	A	O
A	A	Y	A	M	N	I	P	A	Y	G	T
L	P	E	N	C	I	L	C	A	S	E	B
C	A	L	A	A	C	E	P	A	P	E	A
U	R	A	N	G	E	P	E	N	S	O	L
L	D	I	A	R	Y	H	X	U	A	M	L
A	M	O	B	C	I	O	P	H	O	O	S
T	A	P	O	R	A	N	G	E	R	N	E
O	R	A	N	R	Z	E	R	A	S	E	R
R	S	S	A	N	D	W	I	C	H	Y	H

2 ⊙ **12** (Circle) **the correct words. Then listen and check.**

Amy   Hi, ¹ (I'm) / she's Amy.
Poppy Hi, ² I'm / you're Poppy. ³ Is / Are you in my class?
Amy   Yes, I ⁴ am / is. This is David. ⁵ He's / She's in your class, too.
Poppy Hi, David.
David Hello.
Amy   That's Jack and Emma. ⁶ We're / They're brother and sister.
Poppy ⁷ Is / Are they in our class?
David Jack isn't in our class, but Emma is.
Poppy How old ⁸ is / are Jack?
David He's twelve.

Chat zone

⊙ **13** **Complete the conversations with the expressions. Then listen and check.**

Silly me!   See you!   Cool.   I'm late!

1 **Tony**   It's seven o'clock, Joe!
   Joe   Oh no! ....

2 **Leon**   Where are you from?
   Aisha   India.
   Leon   ....

3 **Mike**   Where's my pencil case?
   Josh   Look! It's on your desk.
   Mike   ....

4 **Jordan** Bye!
   Amy   Bye! ....

be – negative

1 Change the sentences to the negative form.

1 We're late for school.
   We aren't late for school.

2 My brother is a student.

....

3 She's from Australia.

....

4 My trainers are in the living room.

....

5 You're in my class.

....

6 I'm in bed.

....

7 It's eight o'clock.

....

8 We're in Class 7B.

....

be – questions and short answers

2 Circle the correct words.

1 .... her name Carmen?
   a Am **b** Is **c** Are

2 .... I in the photo?
   a Am **b** Is **c** Are

3 .... your parents at home?
   a Am **b** Is **c** Are

4 .... we friends?
   a Am **b** Is **c** Are

5 .... your favourite team Real Madrid?
   a Am **b** Is **c** Are

6 .... she nice?
   a Am **b** Is **c** Are

3 Reorder the words to make questions.

1 she / from France / is ?
   Is she from France?

2 your parents / are / British ?

3 I / am / in your class ?

4 your favourite team / Boca Juniors / is ?

5 are / good students / we ?

6 it / a good film / is ?

4 Complete the table for you.

	Age	From	Favourite colour
Harry	13	Manchester	red
Emily	12	London	blue
You			

5 Look at the table in Exercise 4. Answer the questions.

1 Is Harry fourteen?
   No, he isn't. He's thirteen.

2 Is Emily twelve?

....

3 Are you from Mexico City?

....

4 Is your favourite colour pink?

....

5 Is Emily from Dublin?

....

6 Is her favourite colour blue?

....

7 Is Harry from Manchester?

....

8 Is his favourite colour blue?

....

6 Answer the questions for you. Give short answers.

1 Are you good at sport?

....

2 Are you hungry?

....

3 Are you twelve?

....

4 Are you Greek?

....

5 Are you a teacher?

....

6 Is your favourite colour blue?

....

7 Complete with the verb *be*.

1 _Are_ you English? Yes, I _am_ .
2 _____ Ella your sister? No, she _____ .
3 _____ you in my class? Yes, we _____ .
4 _____ your parents from London? Yes, they _____ .
5 _____ it your birthday today? Yes, it _____ .
6 _____ you from Istanbul? No, I _____ not.

8 Write questions with these words. Then write positive or negative answers.

1 she / from the USA (✗ / UK)
Is she from the USA?
No, she isn't. She's from the UK.

2 he / twelve (✗ / eleven)
_____

3 they / in the football team (✓)
_____

4 it / November (✗ / December)
_____

5 they / in the café (✗ / living room)
_____

Articles

9 Write the words in the correct column.

> apple banana computer egg ice cream
> door map friend eraser exercise book
> airport T-shirt umbrella radio animal pen

a	an
banana	apple

Communication

⊙ **14** Complete the conversations. Then listen and check.

> this goodbye I'm thanks nice you hello are you thanks

It's Saturday

A

Mrs Baines	Hi, Ben. Come in.
Ben	¹_____ , Mrs Baines.
Jacob	Hi, Ben. How ²_____ _____ ?
Ben	Fine, thanks. And you?
Jacob	³_____ OK, ⁴_____ .

B

Jacob	Ben, ⁵_____ is Simona.
Ben	Hi, Simona.
Simona	Hello, Ben. ⁶_____ to meet ⁷_____ .
Ben	Where are you from, Simona?
Simona	I'm from Venice in Italy.
Ben	Wow!

C

Ben	Goodbye. ⁸_____ for a nice lunch, Mrs Baines.
Mrs Baines	You're welcome, Ben. ⁹_____ .

Reading and listening

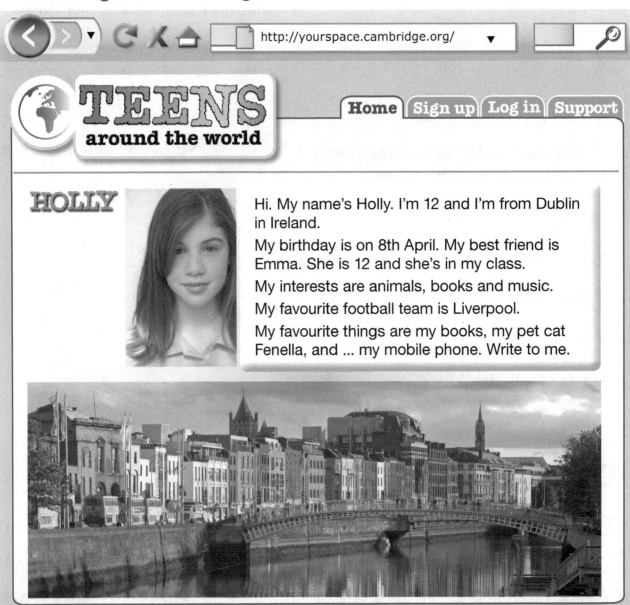

http://yourspace.cambridge.org/

TEENS around the world

Home | Sign up | Log in | Support

HOLLY

Hi. My name's Holly. I'm 12 and I'm from Dublin in Ireland.

My birthday is on 8th April. My best friend is Emma. She is 12 and she's in my class.

My interests are animals, books and music.

My favourite football team is Liverpool.

My favourite things are my books, my pet cat Fenella, and ... my mobile phone. Write to me.

1 Read about Holly and complete the table.

	Holly	Kevin
Age	....	....
Birthday	8th	.....................th November
From	Dublin, ...	Paris, ...
Interests	animals, ... and	computer games, ... and ....
Favourite football team	....	PSG
Favourite things	....................., pet cat, ...	football shirt, ...
Best friend	....	....

2 🔘 15 Listen to Kevin and complete the table above.

Writing

3 Complete the table for you.

	You
Age	
Birthday	
From	
Interests	
Favourite football team	
Favourite things	
Best friend	

your photo

4 Write a paragraph about you. Use the information from Exercise 3.

Hi. My name's _____

_____

_____

_____

_____

Your progress

Look at Student's Book Unit 1. Circle: ☹ = not very well ☺ = quite well 😎 = very well

I can give personal information about my age, nationality and family.	☹ ☺ 😎	p19
I can give personal information about my friend.	☹ ☺ 😎	p23
I can read and can understand information about people.	☹ ☺ 😎	p26
I can listen and understand simple personal information.	☹ ☺ 😎	p27
I can write simple sentences about me and my life.	☹ ☺ 😎	p27
I can introduce friends and use basic greetings.	☹ ☺ 😎	p118

Your project: a tourism poster

- Choose a country. Find these facts:
  the population   the flag   the capital city   the money   the language(s)
- Find some interesting facts about the country. Choose from:
  national emblem   tourist sites   weather   sports
  famous people   interesting facts
- Find or draw a map and pictures. Use the internet to help you.
- Make your poster. Give it a title and stick on the map and pictures.
  Write your facts.

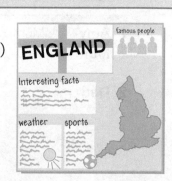

1 Look at the pictures and write the rooms.

1 __bathroom__   2 _____   3 _____   4 _____   5 _____

2 Where are the people? Look at the pictures and write sentences.

1 Zoe (MORDBEO)   **2** Dan (ECNTIKH)   **3** Mel (RENGDA)   **4** Leo (INNDIGMOOR)
Zoe is in the bedroom   _____   _____   _____

3   ◎ 16   Complete the conversations. Then listen and check.

> I am   it isn't   are you   we aren't

1	**Mum**	Hurry up. It's late.	
	Liam	_____ late. It's early.	

3 Callum   _____ in the kitchen, Dad?
Dad   No, I'm not.

2 Ella   We're late for school.
Laura   No, _____ . It's Sunday.

4 Mum   Are you in the bathroom, Jake?
Jake   Yes, _____ .

Chat zone

◎ 17   Complete the conversations with the expressions. Then listen and check.

> Come in   I don't know.   Hurry up!   What's so funny?

1 Amy   Mum, are you in your bedroom?
Mum   Yes. _____ , Amy.

3 Oliver   Ha ha ha!
George   _____

2 Dad   _____ You're late.

4 Lucy   Where's Zoe?
Tom   _____

Question words and *be*

1 Complete the questions with the question words. Then write answers for you.

1 _What_ is your name? My name is ...
2 _____ is your birthday?
3 _____ is your favourite actor?
4 _____ old are you?
5 _____ are you from?
6 _____ time is it?
7 _____ is your teacher?
8 _____ is your phone number?

2 🔘 18 Listen and complete the conversations with question words and *be*. Then match with the pictures.

1 Ben _What's_ her name?
   Tom Her name's Lauren.
   Ben _____ she from?
   Tom She's from the USA.

2 Sam _____ you?
   Ana I'm twelve.
   Sam _____ your birthday?
   Ana Tomorrow!

3 Sue _____ your favourite pop star?
   Tim Leona Lewis.
   Sue _____ your favourite food?
   Tim Chocolate!

4 Lea _____ they from?
   Rob They're from India.
   Lea _____ old _____ they?
   Rob She's eleven and he's fourteen.

a
b
c
d

3 Match the questions and answers.

1 Who is your favourite singer? [e]
2 What is his name? [ ]
3 When is your birthday? [ ]
4 What are his interests? [ ]
5 Where are they from? [ ]
6 How old is your brother? [ ]

a He's sixteen.
b They're from Brazil.
c His name's Luis.
d It's today!
e It's Shakira.
f Football and computers.

4 Complete the sentences with *there is*, *there are*, *there isn't* or *there aren't*.

1 _There is_ a computer on my desk. (✓)
2 _____ two pens in your pencil case. (✗)
3 _____ a river in London. (✓)
4 _____ 15 computers in the computer room. (✓)
5 _____ a football team at my school. (✗)
6 _____ a café in my school. (✗)

5 **Look at the picture and write questions and answers.**

1 two windows
Are there two windows? No, there aren't. There are three windows.

2 a phone
Is there a phone? No, there isn't.

3 three computers

....

4 ten chairs

....

5 two teachers

....

6 a map

....

7 five students

....

8 a TV

....

lots of

6 **Complete the sentences with *a*, *an* or *lots of*.**

1 There are <u>lots of</u> students in my class.
2 There's .... cinema in my street.
3 There are .... people in London.
4 There's .... teacher from England at my school.
5 There are .... pens in my pencil case.
6 There are .... windows in my house.
7 There's .... umbrella in the hall.
8 There are .... books in the study.

Plurals

7 **Complete the *spidergrams* with plurals of these words.**

~~foot~~ ~~box~~ ~~toy~~ ~~baby~~ student woman
pencil glass person diary man book
guitar beach child strawberry

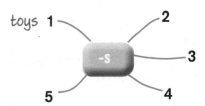

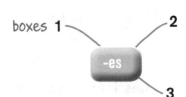

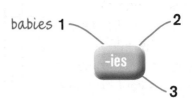

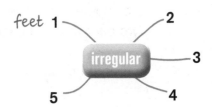

1 Complete the crossword.

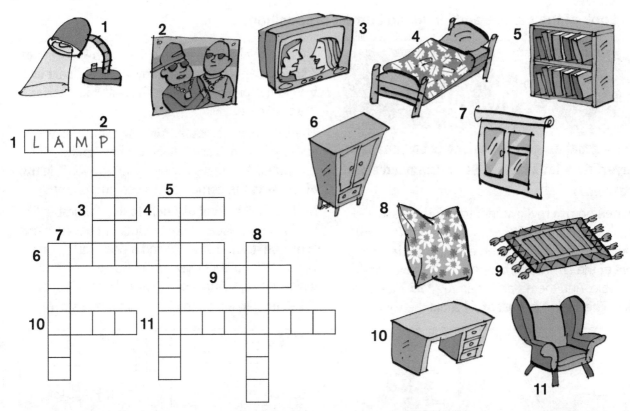

1 L A M P

2 Look at the pictures and read the sentences. Match the sentences with the rooms.

| A | B |

1 There is an armchair. ...A...
2 There are two posters. ....
3 There is one cushion. ....
4 There are two windows. ....

5 There is a TV. ....
6 There isn't a rug. ....
7 There isn't a computer. ....
8 There is a girl! ....

Chat zone

🔘 **19** Complete the conversations with the expressions. Then listen and check.

It's a mess!   stuff   Oh dear!

1 Joe   There's lots of ....
in my room. Books, CDs, T-shirts,
posters.

2 Tina   ....
We're late for school.

3 Rob   Don't look at my room!
....

Prepositions of place

1 Look at the picture and circle the correct preposition.

CELEBRITY HOMES

He's a great singer. His music is on your mp3 player. Now let's look at Scott Diamond's cool bedroom.

My bedroom is my favourite room. There's lots of space for my friends! There's a table ¹ **in front of** / **behind** the sofa. And there's a lamp ² **behind** / **in front of** the armchair. There are DVDs ³ **on** / **under** the table. And there's an Indian rug ⁴ **on** / **under** the table. The TV is ⁵ **in front of** / **behind** the window.

Music is my life. There's a white piano ⁶ **in front of** / **behind** the wardrobe and my guitar is ⁷ **next to** / **behind** the piano. My music CDs are ⁸ **in** / **under** the bookcase.

There's a new computer ⁹ **in** / **on** the desk. My computer games are ¹⁰ **behind** / **next to** the computer. And that's my new mp3 player ¹¹ **in front of** / **next to** the computer. It's very important!

My bed is ¹² **in front of** / **next to** the wardrobe. It's my favourite place. There are lots of cool cushions ¹³ **in** / **on** it. I'm a student and a pop star! I'm not a good student! Look! My school books are ¹⁴ **on** / **under** the bed. And look at my collection of trainers ¹⁵ **behind** / **in** the wardrobe. What a mess!

this, *that*, *these*, *those*

2 Complete the sentences with *this*, *that*, *these* or *those* and the verb *be*.

1

This is
my cat.

2

_____
my school.

3

_____
my trainers.

4

_____
my school books.

5

_____
my computer.

6

_____
my friends.

3 Complete the questions with *this/that/ these/those* and the answers with *It's* or *They're*.

1

What are <u>those</u> ?
<u>They're</u> cushions.

2

What's .... ?
.... a bookcase.

3

What's .... ?
.... a cat.

4

What are ....?
.... T-shirts.

Possessive adjectives

4 Complete the sentences with possessive adjectives.

1 Look at this photo! It's ...my.......... English friend.

2 This is Jack and .... brother Luke.

3 Isabel is happy. She's in Class 7C with .... friend Zoe.

4 Oscar and Joe are in Class 7A. .... teacher is Mr Elliot.

5 **Holly** What's .... name?
Dylan It's Dylan.

6 **Katie** Ruby, this is .... ice cream.
Ruby Thanks.

7 **Mrs Smith** Hello, Lily. How are .... parents?
Lily Fine, thanks.

8 **Toby and Sophie** .... parents are from Germany.

Communication

◉ 20 Complete the conversation. Then listen and check.

what's   nationality   old   address   family   first   can

At a Youth Club

Sophie Hi! Can I join the Youth Club, please?

Oscar Of course. Can I ask you some questions?

Sophie Yes, sure.

Oscar How ¹ .... are you?

Sophie I'm twelve.

Oscar Good. What's your ² .... name?

Sophie Sophie.

Oscar What's your ³ .... name?

Sophie Brown.

Oscar What's your ⁴ .... ?

Sophie It's 56 Young Street, Cambridge, CB1 2LZ.

Oscar ⁵ .... your phone number?

Sophie It's 01223 76512.

Oscar Sorry, ⁶ .... you repeat that, please?

Sophie 01223 76512.

Oscar Thanks. What's your ⁷ .... ?

Sophie I'm British.

Oscar Great.

Reading

1 Match the words with the pictures.

door ☐ window ☐ swimming pool ☐
lake ☐ helicopter ☐ party ☐

1  2

3  4  5  6

2 Read the article and match the headings with the text.

1 ☐E A special ceremony   3 ☐ A famous balcony   5 ☐ Lots of animals and plants
2 ☐ Lots of people   4 ☐ A very big home

WELCOME TO THE QUEEN'S HOME, BUCKINGHAM PALACE, LONDON

A There are 775 rooms, including 240 bedrooms and 78 bathrooms. There are 1,514 doors and 760 windows. There's a post office, a swimming pool and a cinema. Outside there is a big garden with a lake, and a helicopter park.

B The Queen has special dinners and parties. There are 50,000 visitors each year! The Prime Minister of the UK meets the Queen on Thursdays. Her visitors include Barack and Michelle Obama.

C The Royal Family stand on their famous balcony.

D There are lots of dogs at Buckingham Palace. And there are 30 kinds of birds and 350 kinds of flowers in the garden.

E At 11.30 am every day there is a special ceremony – the Changing of the Guard. It's very popular with tourists.

3 Complete the table.

BUCKINGHAM PALACE IN NUMBERS!	
rooms	775
bedrooms	
bathrooms	
doors	
windows	

4 (Circle) the correct words.

1 Buckingham Palace is in **Liverpool / London**.
2 It is very **big / small**.
3 There is a **swimming pool / school**.
4 There is a famous **balcony / cinema**.
5 There are lots of **cats / dogs**.
6 At **10.30 / 11.30** am there is a special ceremony.

Listening

5 🔘 **21** **Look at the plans. Then listen and write the numbers.**

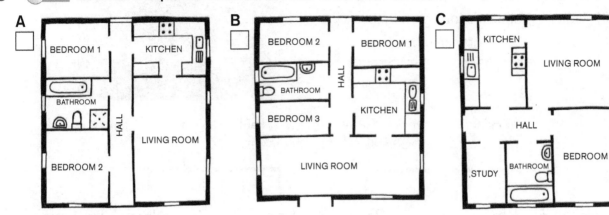

Writing

6 **You are a pop star. Write about your home. Use the ideas in the box.**

MY NAME: ....
There are .... [number] rooms in my home.
There is/are .... [list the rooms].
Outside there is/are .... [list the places].
In my living room there is/are ....
[list the things].

ROOMS
a games room   a music room   a cinema
OUTSIDE
a garden   a swimming pool   a helicopter park
LIVING ROOM
armchair   table   a piano
a big TV   lots of cushions
lots of windows   lots of dogs/cats

Your progress

Look at Student's Book Unit 2. Circle: ☹ = **not very well** ☺ = **quite well** 😎 = **very well**

I can talk about my life and ask and answer simple questions.	☹ ☺ 😎	p29
I can describe a room.	☹ ☺ 😎	p33
I can read and understand an article about homes.	☹ ☺ 😎	p36
I can listen and understand information about homes.	☹ ☺ 😎	p37
I can write a description of a house.	☹ ☺ 😎	p39
I can ask for and give personal information.	☹ ☺ 😎	p119

Your project: a dream room

- You are famous. Draw a picture of your bedroom, or use photos from magazines and make a collage.
- Include: *bed, table, desk, TV, computer, window, chair, armchair, rug, bookcase, wardrobe, lamp, posters, cushions.*
- Add one special thing, for example *a balcony, an aquarium.*
- Label the things and describe them. *This is my ... These are my ...*
- Remember to describe their position. *The TV is next to the bed.*
- Present your dream room to the class.

3A ▦ I've got four cousins

1 Here is Anna's family. Complete the family tree with these words.

| father   brother   aunt   grandfather |
| cousin   uncle   grandmother |

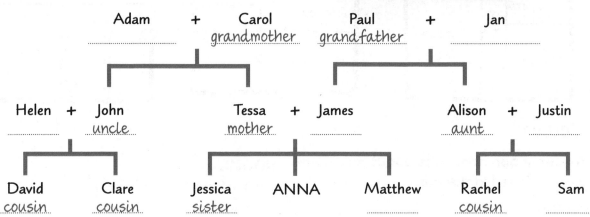

Adam + Carol
.... grandmother

Paul + Jan
grandfather ....

Helen + John
.... uncle

Tessa + James
mother

Alison + Justin
aunt ....

David
cousin

Clare
cousin

Jessica
sister

ANNA

Matthew

Rachel
cousin

Sam

2 Write the missing words.

| 🚹 | son | brother | | | | grandfather |
| 🚺 | daughter | | wife | cousin | aunt | |

3 Draw pictures of people in your family. Then write sentences.

This is my uncle. His name's Paolo.

4 Match the words.

1 (mum) [c]   **2** (dad) [ ]   **3** (auntie) [ ]   **4** (grandad) [ ]   **5** (gran) [ ]

a (aunt)   **b** (grandmother)   **c** (mother)   **d** (father)   **e** (grandfather)

have got – positive

1 Write the sentences again using short forms.

1 I have got three grandparents.
I've got three grandparents.

2 We have got seven cousins!
....

3 She has got one brother.
....

4 You have got a very big family!
....

5 He has got two sisters and one brother.
....

6 They have got a very nice uncle.
....

7 It has got four legs.
....

8 You have got new bikes.
....

9 I have got an mp3 player.
....

10 They have got a big house.
....

2 Write sentences about the people. Use full forms.

Nick

Josh

Mel

Alice

Tim

1 Mel and Tim ...*have*... ...*got*...
...*mobile*... ...*phones*... .

2 Nick .... an mp3
player and a computer.

3 Mel .... a cat, a
computer and a ....

4 Alice .... an
.... and a mobile phone.

5 Tim and Alice ....
....

6 Josh .... a camera
and a ....

7 Tim .... a mobile
phone and a ....

8 Nick and Mel ....
....

Possessive 's

3 Complete the sentences with the correct form of the possessive 's.

1  These are my
brother's (brother)
computer games.

4  This is your
.... (sister)
pencil case.

2  This is my
.... (mother)
mobile phone.

5  These are my
....
(grandmother) cats.

3  These are my
.... (uncle)
photos.

6  This is your
.... (cousin)
book.

4 Look at the pictures and write sentences.

~~computer~~   ~~trainers~~   burgers   mobile phone   books   guitar   T-shirt   mp3 players

Jill and Jenny

Lucia

David

Jake and Leo

1 It's David's computer.
2 They're Jake and Leo's trainers.
3 ....
4 ....

5 ....
6 ....
7 ....
8 ....

1 Put the letters in the right order to find the adjectives.

ROEISSU   ~~RELVCE~~   NUNYF   HYS   DIKN   DRYNFELI

1 My brother Joe is __clever__ .

2 My grandmother is very _____ .

3 My friend Ben is _____ .

4 My cousin George is _____ .

5 My sister Clare is _____ .

6 My friend Becky is very _____ .

2 ◎ **22** Complete the conversations. Then listen and check.

is   haven't   T-shirt   thanks   mine   ~~trainers~~

1

Kate Whose are these ¹ __trainers__ ?

Simon They're ² _____ .

Kate You're joking! They're horrible.

2

Harry Is this ¹ _____ yours?

Jane Yes, it ² _____ .

Harry Well, I think it's silly!

3

Sophie Oh, no! I ¹ _____ got my pen!

Holly Don't worry. Here's mine.

Sophie Oh ² _____ , Holly.

Chat zone

◎ **23** Complete the conversations with the expressions. Then listen and check.

You're joking!   Don't worry.   You're a star!

1 Dave I've got an exam this afternoon.

Mark _____

2 Lucy What's your mobile phone number?

Ana I haven't got a mobile phone.

Lucy _____

3 John I'm hungry.

William Here's a banana.

John _____

have got – negative

1 Circle the correct form.

1 He **hasn't** / **haven't** got a big car.

2 Oh no! I **hasn't** / **haven't** got my school bag.

3 We **hasn't** / **haven't** got new mobile phones.

4 They **hasn't** / **haven't** got bicycles.

5 She **hasn't** / **haven't** got a small family.

6 He **hasn't** / **haven't** got a sandwich for lunch!

2 **Make the sentences negative. Use short forms.**

1 She's got a horse.
She hasn't got a horse.

2 He's got a new skateboard.

....

3 They've got a swimming pool.

....

4 I've got a blue bicycle.

....

5 We've got a DVD player.

....

6 Daniele's got an old computer.

....

7 You've got a black and white cat.

....

3 **Write questions and short answers.**

1 Lily / a brother?
Has Lily got a brother?
Yes, she has.

2 you / lots of books?

....

3 Ruby / a computer?

....................................

4 you / a sister?

....

5 your parents / a car?

....

6 we / a new teacher?

....

Possessive pronouns and *Whose...?*

4 Complete the conversations with the correct possessive pronouns.

| his   ours   mine   theirs |

1

A Whose bicycle is this? Is it yours?
B No, it isn't .... My bicycle is
at home.

3

A Whose guitar is this? Is it Adam's?
B No, it isn't .... Adam's guitar is
black.

2

A Is that your aunt and uncle's car?
B No, it isn't .... Their car is that
red one.

4

A Hey, you two! These are your mobile phones!
B and C They aren't .... Look!

Communication

1 ◎ **24** **Try and say these email
addresses. Then listen and repeat.**

1 harry.jones@blue.net
2 tina.t@abc.com
3 lucy@myhouse.net
4 clark-tom@greenpark.co.uk

2 **Reorder the sentences in the
conversation.**

Lily our project / I've got / information /
some / for
*I've got some information for our
project.*

Matt Fantastic! / email it / can you /
to me / ?

Lily what's your / sure / email address / ?

Matt whitespot@theworld.it / it's

Lily White spot? / one / is that / word / ?

Matt is / it / yes

3 ◎ **25** **Complete the conversation.
Then listen and check.**

Alfie I've got a great photo of you. It's on
my computer at home.

Jess ¹ .... you email it to me?

Alfie Sure. What's your ² ....
address?

Jess ³ .... jesswood@freetime.co.uk.

Alfie Sorry, can you ⁴ .... that again,
please?

Jess Sure. It's jesswood@freetime.co.uk.

Alfie Is that one ⁵ .... ?

Jess Yes, it is.

Reading and listening

1 🔘 **26** **Listen and complete the email.**

tall   short   dark   kind   slim   funny   clever   ~~long~~   fashion   sixteen

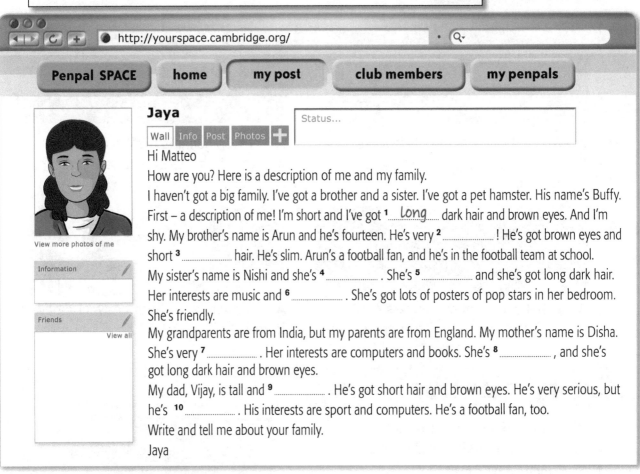

Penpal SPACE   home   **my post**   club members   my penpals

Jaya

Status...

Wall | Info | Post | Photos | ✚

Hi Matteo

How are you? Here is a description of me and my family.

I haven't got a big family. I've got a brother and a sister. I've got a pet hamster. His name's Buffy.

First – a description of me! I'm short and I've got ¹ ....*Long*.... dark hair and brown eyes. And I'm shy. My brother's name is Arun and he's fourteen. He's very ² .... ! He's got brown eyes and short ³ .... hair. He's slim. Arun's a football fan, and he's in the football team at school.

My sister's name is Nishi and she's ⁴ .... She's ⁵ .... and she's got long dark hair. Her interests are music and ⁶ .... She's got lots of posters of pop stars in her bedroom. She's friendly.

My grandparents are from India, but my parents are from England. My mother's name is Disha. She's very ⁷ .... Her interests are computers and books. She's ⁸ .... , and she's got long dark hair and brown eyes.

My dad, Vijay, is tall and ⁹ .... He's got short hair and brown eyes. He's very serious, but he's ¹⁰ .... His interests are sport and computers. He's a football fan, too.

Write and tell me about your family.

Jaya

2 **Read the email and label the pictures with their names.**

Jaya   Arun   ~~Vijay~~   Nishi   Disha

1 ...Vijay...   2 ....   3 ....   4 ....   5 ....

3 Read the email and decide if the sentences are true (*T*) or false (*F*).
Correct the false ones.

1 Jaya has got two brothers and one sister. _F_ - *Jaya has got one brother and one sister.*
2 She has got short dark hair and brown eyes. ....
3 Arun is 14 and he's plump. ....
4 Jaya's sister is tall and she's got long dark hair. ....
5 Disha's interests are computers and sport. ....
6 Arun and Vijay are football fans. ....

Writing

4 Complete the table for two members of your family.

	Name	Name ....
Age		
Build		
Eye colour		
Hair type		
Hair colour		
Interests		

5 Write descriptions of the people in Exercise 4. Use Jaya's email as a model.

Your progress

Look at Student's Book Unit 3. Circle: ☹ = not very well ☺ = quite well 😁 = very well

I can describe my family.	☹	☺	😁	p38
I can ask and answer simple questions about possessions.	☹	☺	😁	p42
I can talk about my possessions.	☹	☺	😁	p43
I can read and understand simple descriptions of people.	☹	☺	😁	p47
I can write a description of people I know.	☹	☺	😁	p47
I can ask for and give an email address.	☹	☺	😁	p120

Your project: guess the person

• Make a poster with two photos of people from the internet or a magazine.
  Number the photos.
• Make two cards and write a description of one person on each card. Write about:
     build   eye colour   hair type   hair colour
• Put all your posters on the classroom wall. Put all the cards together. The class
  guesses which person the cards describe.

1 Complete the actions in the daily routine.

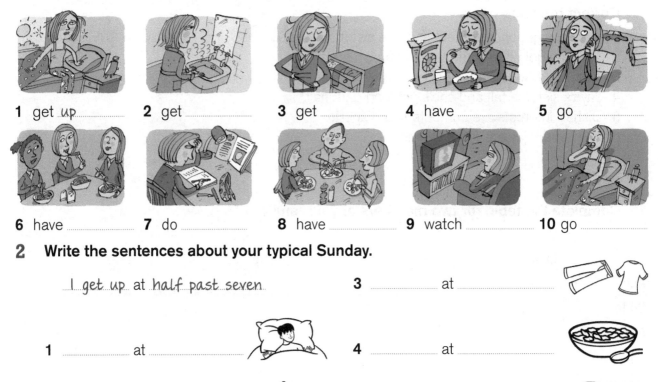

1 get up .... 2 get .... 3 get .... 4 have .... 5 go ....

6 have .... 7 do .... 8 have .... 9 watch .... 10 go ....

2 Write the sentences about your typical Sunday.

I get up at half past seven

3 .... at ....

1 .... at ....

4 .... at ....

2 .... at ....

5 .... at ....

3 🔘 **27** Put the sentences in the right order. Then listen and check.

A day in the life of Abigail

**My name is Abigail and I'm 13.
I live in Brighton. And this is my routine.**

We have dinner at quarter to seven. ⸂8⸃

I have breakfast at half past seven. I have cereal (cornflakes), an apple and a glass of milk. ☐

After school I do my homework in my bedroom (and listen to music). ☐

I have lunch at school at half past twelve. My favourite lunch is fish and chips. ☐

I get up at quarter past seven in the morning. ☐

I go to school with my best friend Zara. ☐

School finishes at quarter past three and I go home with Zara. ☐

I go to bed at ten o'clock and go to sleep at five past ten. ☐

Then I get washed and get dressed. ☐

In the evening I play computer games or watch TV with my family. ☐

Present simple – positive

1 Write the third person singular form of the verbs in the correct column.

~~play~~ watch buy go read start tidy
finish cry do wash listen carry

-s	-es	-ies
plays		

2 Complete the sentences with the correct form of the verb. Then match with the pictures.

1 I _play_ computer games after dinner. (play) [e]

2 My sister _____ TV before breakfast. (watch) [ ]

3 We _____ to the supermarket on Saturday. (go) [ ]

4 Jacopo and Michele _____ their homework in the evening. (do) [ ]

5 Jack _____ lots of books. (buy) [ ]

6 Dad _____ the car every week. (wash) [ ]

a

d

b

e

c

f

3 Match the days with the activities and write sentences about Dan's week.

have pizza   watch films   play football
read magazines   listen to music
~~wash the dog~~   tidy his room

Monday
Tuesday
Wednesday
Thursday
Friday
Saturday
Sunday

1 _Dan washes the dog on Monday._

2 _____

3 _____

4 _____

5 _____

6 _____

7 _____

4 Write sentences for you and your family. Choose from the verbs below.

| get up   go   play   start   meet |
| finish   watch   eat   study |

My brother plays football on Saturday

Me and my family

1 .... on Monday.

2 .... on Tuesday.

3 .... on Wednesday

4 .... on Thursday

5 .... on Friday.

6 .... on Saturday.

7 .... on Sunday.

Prepositions of time

5 Write the time expressions next to the pictures.

| in the evening   in the afternoon |
| at night   in the morning |

1  ....

2  ....

3  ....

4  ....

6 Write the times with the expressions.

1 half past six
in the morning

2  ....
in the evening

3  ....
in the afternoon

4  ....
in the morning

5  ....
at night

6 ....
in the evening

7  ....
in the afternoon

8  ....
in the morning

7 Write the times with a time expression.

1 15.15 It's quarter past three
in the afternoon.

2 22.20 ....

3 01.30 ....

4 16.55 ....

5 09.05 ....

6 11.20 ....

1 🔘 **28** **Look at the pictures and write what the people do on Saturday. Then listen and check.**

1 I play football

2 We

3 I

4 We

5 I

6 We

2 **Add the words to the spidergrams. Some words go in more than one place.**

letters   a blog   board games   books   computer games   text messages   emails

letters

 send

 write

letters  read

 play

3 🔘 **29** **Match the questions and the replies. Then listen and check.**

1 Do you watch TV in the evening?

2 Does your sister write poems?

3 What does your mum do in her free time?

4 Does your brother play computer games?

5 Do your parents go shopping on Saturday?

6 Do you send text messages?

a No, he doesn't. And he doesn't surf the web.

b Yes, I do. I send them to all my friends.

c No, she doesn't. But she reads poems.

d She plays the piano and reads magazines.

e No, I don't. I listen to music and I write a blog.

f Yes, they do.

Chat zone

🔘 **30** **Complete the conversations with the expressions. Then listen and check**

Me too!   What about ...   Follow me.   Like you.

1 Ben Do you surf the web?
Dan Yes, and I play computer games ...
_____

2 Andy I love pizzas.
Jason _____

3 Adam I love all the Spider-Man films.
Grace _____ the Batman films?
Adam I love them, too!

4 Ellie Excuse me. Where's the music room?
Teacher _____

Present simple – negative

1 Match the sentences with the pictures.

1 David doesn't like fish.
2 My friends don't play football.
3 Rachel doesn't go to bed early on Saturday night.
4 Joe and Anna don't walk to school.
5 Jasmine doesn't watch TV.
6 Ian doesn't do his homework in the evening.

a ☐ b ☐
c ☐ d ☐
e [1] f ☐

2 Make the sentences negative. Use short forms.

1 My parents watch The Simpsons.
My parents don't watch The Simpsons.
2 My sister lives in Madrid.
3 You get up early at the weekend.
4 Omar has his lunch at school.
5 I take photos with my mobile phone.
6 They visit their grandparents on Sunday.
7 We send text messages at school.

Present simple – questions and short answers

3 Circle the correct words.

1 **Do / Does** Connor have coffee for breakfast?
2 **Do / Does** you go to bed early?
3 **Do / Does** we have a Science lesson today?
4 **Do / Does** your grandmother like animals?
5 **Do / Does** Olivia and John go to school on the same bus?
6 **Do / Does** you understand this question?

4 Write the words in the correct order to make questions.

1 collect / you / things / do ?
Do you collect things?
2 play / Ronaldo / does / Brazil / for ?
3 English / mum / speak / your / does ?
4 an / you / do / in / apartment / live ?
5 Monday / to / we / school / do / on / walk ?
6 they / messages / text / do / send ?

5 Write sentences about Charlie and Hannah.

	Charlie	Hannah
speak French	✗	✗
play the guitar	✓	✗
surf the web	✓	✓
walk to school	✗	✓

1 Charlie and Hannah *don't speak French.*
2 Charlie
3 Hannah
4 Charlie and Hannah
5 Charlie
6 Hannah

6 Complete the table for you. Then write
sentences.

	You
speak Spanish	
play the piano	
eat fast food	
watch football	
listen to music	
drink milk	

I don't speak Spanish.
I play the piano.

1 ....

2 ....

3 ....

4 ....

5 ....

6 ....

Communication

Summer Fun

July 12th–13th New Park
For tickets call 01457 652290

live pop music, food,
games and fun!

1 Read the advert and answer the questions.

1 What is Summer Fun? ....

2 Where is it? ....

3 When is it? ....

4 Why do you call 01457 652290?
....

2 🔘 **31** Complete the conversations with these words. Then listen and check.

help like that's tickets time can start here much

Woman   Hello, ¹ .... I ² .... you?

Zoe   Yes, please. What ³ .... does Summer Fun ⁴ .... ?

Woman   It starts at 11 o'clock in the morning.

Zoe   How ⁵ .... are the tickets?

Woman   Well, for children up to sixteen years it's £4 and for adults it's £9.

Zoe   Oh, that's good. I'm eleven. I'd ⁶ .... three tickets, please – two adults and
one child.

Woman   ⁷ .... £22, please.

Zoe   ⁸ .... you are.

Woman   Here are your ⁹ .... and your change.

Reading

1   **Match the words to the pictures.**

farm ☐4☐   hat ☐   rodeo ☐   cow ☐   horse ☐   fire ☐   tent ☐

1   2   3   4   5   6   7

---

http://yourspace.cambridge.org/

CHAD'S WORK BLOG

A day in the life of a cowboy

Hi! I'm Chad. I'm a cowboy in Montana, USA. I work on a big
farm with ten other cowboys. The farm has got 3,000 cows.
In the summer I sleep in a tent. I get up very early, at 5 am.
We cook breakfast on a fire. After breakfast I get ready. Then
I ride with the other cowboys to the 'cow camp'.

Let me tell you about my job. In the winter we give food to the cows. In the spring there are lots of
calves (baby cows). In the summer we move the cows to new places every day. We work 16 hours a
day in the summer. But on Thursdays we ride in the rodeo. That's fun!

I'm very tired in the evening. But before dinner I clean my horse and give him his dinner. He's very
important! Then I get washed and I have dinner with the other cowboys. We eat lots of meat and
potatoes and drink coffee.

A cowboy's life is dangerous but I love my job. And I love my horse. I don't wear a uniform but I
wear jeans and a cowboy shirt. And I've got a big cowboy hat, of course!

2   **Read Chad's blog and answer the questions with short answers.**
    Correct the wrong information.

1   Does he work in an office? No, he doesn't. He works outside on a farm.

2   Does he sleep in his bedroom? ....

3   Does he get up early? ....

4   Does he ride a horse? ....

5   Does he work with animals? ....

6   Does he work long hours in the summer? ....

7   Does he eat lots of green vegetables? ....

8   Does he like his job? ....

9   Does he wear a uniform? ....

Listening

3 ⊙ **32** **Listen and guess what the people do. Number the jobs in order.**

doctor ⬚5⬚ bus driver ⬚ shop assistant ⬚ farmer ⬚ office worker ⬚ teacher ⬚

Writing

4 **Look at the example. Write sentences about a person doing one of the jobs in Exercise 3.**

Include this information:

- what the job is
- where he or she works (a hospital / a shop / a farm / an office / a school)
- when he or she starts and finishes work
- what he or she does (drives a bus / works outside / uses a computer / works with animals)
- what he or she wears / doesn't wear (uniform / special clothes)

He's a doctor. He works in a hospital. He starts work at 8 am and finishes at 6 pm. He works with people. He doesn't work with animals. He wears special white clothes.

Your progress

Look at Student's Book Unit 4. Circle: ☹ = not very well ☺ = quite well 😎 = very well

I can read and understand a daily routine.	☹	☺	😎	p49
I can talk about daily routine.	☹	☺	😎	p49
I can give personal information about my interests.	☹	☺	😎	p53
I can read and understand an article about jobs.	☹	☺	😎	p56
I can listen and understand key information about jobs.	☹	☺	😎	p57
I can write a simple description of a job.	☹	☺	😎	p57
I can buy a ticket and talk about numbers and prices.	☹	☺	😎	p121

Your project: free time survey

- Think of 10 weekend activities and write questions, for example:

  At the weekend

  1 Do you play tennis?

- Ask five friends or family members the questions.

  Make a note of their answers: (✓) for Yes and (✗) for No.

- Make a bar graph with the Yes answers.

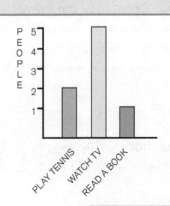

5A Can you swim?

1 Circle ten sports in the word snake. Then match the sports with the pictures.

tennisswimmingbasketballvolleyballcyclingrunningrugbygymnasticsfootballkarate

2 Write the names of the sports under the pictures. Then complete the sentences for you.

1 do _karate_   2 do _____   3 play _____   4 play _____

5 play _____   6 play _____   7 go _____   8 go _____

I play _____
I don't play _____
I do _____
I don't do _____
I go _____
I don't go _____

3 ⊙ **33** Complete the conversations. Then listen and check.

| yes | sports | very | do |
| volleyball | no | can | ~~play~~ |

1 **Henry**   Can you _play_ tennis?
  David   _____ , I can't.

2 **Lily**   Can Lucas _____ karate?
  Emily   _____ , he can. He's amazing!

3 **James**   Can you do any _____ ?
  Amelia   I can play _____ quite well. I can swim _____ well. And I _____ do gymnastics quite well.

Chat zone

⊙ **34** Complete the conversations with the expressions. Then listen and check.

| That's true. | You're amazing! | Sorry. |

1 **Joe**   I can swim five kilometres.
  Ryan   _____

2 **Teacher**   Where's your homework?
  Millie   It's at home. _____

3 **Ella**   Why are you in bed? It's eight o'clock!
  Leon   There's no school today. It's Sunday.
  Ella   _____

can – positive and negative

1 Complete the sentences with *can* or *can't*.

1 Lizzy ..can.. play the piano.
2 Alex .... ride a bike.
3 Lizzy .... sing.
4 Alex .... do karate.

5 Lizzy .... cook spaghetti.
6 Alex and Lizzy .... play tennis.
7 Alex and Lizzy .... swim.
8 Alex and Lizzy .... juggle.

2 Look at the table and complete the sentences about Zara, Billy and Emma. Use *can* or *can't*.

	Zara	Billy	Emma
do gymnastics	✓	✓	✗
speak German	✓	✓	✓
play basketball	✗	✓	✗
ride a horse	✓	✗	✗

1 Zara ..can ride.. a horse but she ..can't play.. basketball.
2 Billy and Zara .... gymnastics.
3 Emma .... German but she .... gymnastics.
4 Zara and Emma .... basketball.
5 Billy .... German but he .... a horse.
6 Zara, Billy and Emma .... German.

3 Match the questions and the answers.

1 Can you play the piano?
2 Can your brother drive?
3 Can Lisa speak Turkish?
4 Can your parents play volleyball?
5 Can you ride a horse?
6 Can Ben and Jake do gymnastics?

a No, she can't. But she can speak Spanish.
b Yes, I can. I love animals.
c Yes, they can. And Ben is brilliant!
d Yes, they can.
e No, I can't. But I can play the guitar.
f Yes, he can.

4 Write questions and short answers.

1 she / read Chinese? (✓)
Can she read Chinese?
Yes, she can.

2 William / play basketball? (✗)
No, he can't.

3 Ahmed and Jamie / play rugby? (✓)

....

4 Molly / dance? (✓)

....

5 you / do judo? (✗)

....

6 your mother / play computer games? (✓)

....

7 you / speak Greek? (✗)

....

8 your grandad / send text messages? (✓)

....

5 Write questions and answers for you.

1  Can you swim?
Yes, I can.

2  ....
....

3  ....
....

4  ....
....

5  ....
....

Adverbs of manner

6 Write sentences about the people in the pictures. Use can, can't and the adverbs.

1  Jason / play tennis / not at all
Jason can't play tennis at all.

2  Lauren / take photos / very well

....

3  They / do karate / quite well

....

4  My dad / dance / not at all

....

5 My gran / use the computer / quite well

....

6 We / sing / very well

....

7 Write sentences with can or can't. Use at all, quite well, very well and these verbs.

speak English   dance   sing   ~~swim~~
ride a horse   juggle   ride a bicycle
play the guitar   play football   ~~cook~~

My father can cook very well.
My grandmother can't swim at all.

1 ....
2 ....
3 ....
4 ....
5 ....
6 ....
7 ....
8 ....

1 Reorder the letters to find words. Then complete the expressions with the words.

1 I T S A G Y N staying in bed

4 K L I A N W G .... in the park

2 E I N D R A G .... books

5 I N S G G N I .... songs

3 I O N G D .... puzzles

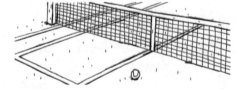

6 N G L Y I A P .... tennis

2 Complete the table for you with activities.

I like 😊	I don't like 🙁

3 🔘 **35** Listen and ⟨circle⟩ the words you hear.

In the morning I hate **¹⟨staying in bed⟩ / getting up**. After school I like playing **² computer games / ball games**. I play them for about **³ half an hour / two hours** a day. I like **⁴ going by car / cycling**. I do **⁵ judo / karate** for about four hours a week.

like / love / hate + -ing

1 Complete these sentences.

love ☺☺   like ☺

don't like ☹   hate ☹☹

	George	Millie	Sam
skiing	☺☺	☺☺	☺
drawing	☺	☹☹	☹☹
cooking	☺☺	☺	☺
singing	☹☹	☺	☺☺

1 _Millie_ likes singing.
2 _George_ and _Millie_ love skiing.
3 .... loves cooking.
4 .... and .... hate drawing.
5 .... likes skiing.
6 .... hates singing.
7 .... and .... like cooking.
8 .... likes drawing.
9 .... loves singing.

2 Write the *-ing* form of the verbs.

1 run _running_ ....
2 study ....
3 write ....
4 take ....
5 go ....
6 swim ....
7 listen ....
8 give ....
9 shop ....
10 have ....
11 buy ....
12 sit ....
13 eat ....
14 dance ....

3 Complete the sentences with the correct form of the verbs.

> watch   drink   shop   study
> ~~play~~   go   have   play

1 My dad loves _playing_ the electric guitar.
2 I don't like .... to bed early.
3 My brother hates .... showers.
4 My friend Ryan doesn't like .... Science.
5 We like .... football after school.
6 Isabella likes .... tea with her breakfast.
7 We hate .... old films on TV.
8 My parents love .... on the internet.

4 Write true sentences for you. Use *love, like, don't like* or *hate.*

1 read books
   I _like reading books._
2 dance
   ....
3 watch TV
   ....
4 swim in the sea
   ....
5 run
   ....
6 send text messages
   ....
7 go to school
   ....
8 eat vegetables
   ....

Imperatives

5 **What do the people say to Oliver? Complete the sentences with the positive or negative form of the verbs.**

use   watch   wash   tidy   ~~wake up~~   walk

1 _Wake up_ , Oliver! You're late!

2 .... on the carpet!

3 .... my computer!

4 .... your hands!

5 .... your room!

6 .... TV!

Communication

🔘 **36** **Complete the conversations. Then listen and check.**

A

Chloe Let's ¹ .... volleyball.

Max I can't play volleyball. ² .... go to my house and ³ .... to music.

Chloe That's a ⁴ .... idea.

B

Max Let's ⁵ .... football in the park.

Connor I'm sorry, I ⁶ .... this evening. I've got a guitar lesson.

Max No problem. ⁷ .... meet on Saturday afternoon.

Connor Yes, that's a good idea.

Reading

1 **Look at the pictures. What sports can you see?**

<u>football</u> ....

2 **Read the article and match the excuses with the paragraphs.**

> I'm not slim.   Sport? Not in my family!   ~~It's not cool!~~
> It's for boys.   I don't like teams.   I get very hot!

Why keep fit?

All across the world teens watch TV, listen to music, play computer games and eat snacks and sweets. But some of them don't exercise. Why not? Let's look at some common excuses.

Excuse 1 (It's not cool.)

Some of our favourite celebrities are sports stars. Think of David Beckham or Maria Sharapova! And look at all those cool young people in the Olympic Games.

Excuse 2 (   )

Be the first person in your family to do a sport! Get your brother or sister or your mum or dad to join you!

Excuse 3 (   )

Lots of girls think this. But girls are good at sport and sport is good for them. Try a different sport. What about dance or judo?

Excuse 4 (   )

It's normal to get hot. All the other players get hot, too!

Excuse 5 (   )

Don't worry. Just enjoy it. Get fit and lose weight.

Excuse 6 (   )

Playing in teams is only one way to get fit. What about swimming, running or walking?

> Sport and exercise are fun. You meet new people and make friends. It's good for your brain, too. It helps with your school work and your computer games! So don't wait! Get some exercise today!

3 **Read the article again and find:**

- three free time activities <u>watch TV</u> ....
- one famous sport competition ....
- two famous people ....
- four family words ....
- five sports ....

Listening

4 🔘 **37** Listen to the sounds and write the number next to the sport.

| a | 1 | | b | | | c | | | d | | | e | | | f | | |

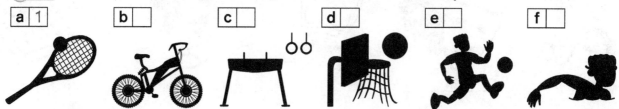

5 Write sentences about each sport.

1 The first sport is tennis.

Writing

6 Complete the sentences about your favourite team sport.

> My favourite team sport is .... There are ....
> players in a team. My favourite team is .... and
> my favourite players are .... and .... I can
> play .... (well, quite well, etc.). I like it because it is
> .... (fun, exciting, etc.).

Your progress

Look at Student's Book Unit 5. Circle: 🙁 = not very well 🙂 = quite well 😎 = very well

I can ask and answer questions about doing sport.	🙁 🙂 😎	p59
I can read and understand words and phrases on signs.	🙁 🙂 😎	p65
I can read and understand simple information about a summer camp.	🙁 🙂 😎	p66
I can listen and understand numbers.	🙁 🙂 😎	p67
I can write and give personal information about free time.	🙁 🙂 😎	p63 & 67
I can make suggestions and arrange to meet.	🙁 🙂 😎	p122

Your project: poetry day

• Make a list:

  sport   place   free time activity   like   don't like

• Then write a poem

About me

• Stick the poem on a card. Decorate the
  card with pictures.

• Have a poetry day. Read out your
  poems in class.

> **About me**
>
> I like football, I can play it very well,
> But I don't like karate, I can't play it at all.
> I like my special sofa, I sit and read all day,
> But I don't like the school bus – it takes me to my school!
> I like my computer games, I play them in my room,
> But I don't like homework, I've got a lot to do!

1 What are the school subjects? Label the pictures.

 1 R E _____

 2 D _____ a

 3 I _ T

 4 G _ o _ r _ phy

 5 M _____ s

 6 A _ t

 7 S _ i _ c _

 8 P E

 9 M _____ ic

 10 L _____ g _____ g _ s

2 Complete the school diary with your lessons.

	Monday	Tuesday	Wednesday	Thursday	Friday	Saturday
Morning						
Afternoon						

3 Match the language with the speaker.

Arabic [6]   Spanish ☐   Russian ☐   German ☐   Turkish ☐   Chinese ☐

| ¡Hola! ¿Como te llamas? | Привет! Тебя как зовут? | 你叫什么名字？ | Merhaba! Adın ne? | Hallo! Wie heißt du? | مرحبا! ما هو اسمك؟ |

 1   2   3   4   5    6

4 38 Match the questions with the answers. Then listen and check.

1 Where is your school?

2 How do you go to school?

3 What lessons do you do on Monday?

4 What do you have for lunch?

5 How many lessons are there?

a I do Maths, Science, English and Art.

b It's in Edinburgh, Scotland.

c I have sandwiches and an orange juice.

d I go to school by bus.

e There are five lessons a day.

Adverbs of frequency

1 Complete the sentences with the correct adverb of frequency.

always	████████	100%
usually	██████	80–99%
often	█████	60–80%
sometimes	███	20–60%
not often	██	1–20%
never		0%

1 Sara ~~usually~~ goes to football practice on Monday. 80–99%

2 Charlie doesn't .... do his homework. 1–20%

3 I am .... late for school. 0%

4 We .... watch TV after dinner. 20–60%

5 Nathan .... has pasta at school. 60–80%

6 My parents .... go shopping on Saturday. 100%

7 They are .... busy at the weekend. 80–99%

8 Natasha .... plays tennis in the afternoon. 20–60%

2 Reorder the words to make sentences.

1 often / my dad / to work / drives
My dad often drives to work.

2 go to / at the weekend / usually / the cinema / we

....

3 never / helps / my brother / my parents

....

4 often / in trouble / I / at school / am

....

5 with / always / my sister / plays / the dog

....

6 computer games / buy / new / doesn't / Vlad / often

....

7 is / at home / she / never / in the evening

....

8 usually / in her bedroom / to music / Laura / listens

....

3 Write sentences about Luka's weekend.

go to the cinema 1—20%
be online 60—80%
play computer games 100%
get up before seven o'clock 0%
meet friends on Saturday 80—99%
send emails to his penpal 60—80%
do his homework on Saturday 20—60%

1 Luka doesn't often go to the cinema.

2 ....

3 ....

4 ....

5 ....

6 ....

7 ....

Prepositions of time

4 Complete the sentences about Sarah with prepositions.

Sarah

1 I always go shopping .... Sunday.

2 I can't work very well .... the morning.

3 My cat often goes out .... night.

4 .... Wednesday we have steak and chips.

5 My birthday is .... the 18th of April.

6 We go to the seaside .... the summer.

7 I always phone my friends .... 8 pm.

8 We often ski .... February.

5 Match the questions and answers.

1 Where do you live?	**a** I usually play football.
2 How do you go to the city centre?	**b** No, I don't.
3 What do you do on Saturday?	**c** Yes, she does.
4 Do you like fish?	**d** At 12.30 pm.
5 Why do you cycle to school?	**e** In Madrid.
6 Does your mum work in an office?	**f** By bus.
7 When does the lesson finish?	**g** Because it's near my home.

6 Circle the correct question word. Then answer the questions for you.

1 Where / Who do you live?

....

2 How / What do you have for breakfast?

....

3 When / Who does your school start?

....

4 What time / How do you get up?

....

5 Whose / Why book is this?

....

6 Which / How do you go home after school?

....

7 Complete the conversation with the correct form of the verb.

Miu	Hi. ¹ Do you come from France? (come)
Pablo	No, I ² .... I'm Spanish. Where ³ .... you .... from? (come)
Miu	I ⁴ .... in Hitachi in Japan. (live) Where ⁵ .... you .... ? (live)
Pablo	I live in Barcelona. It's a big city in the east of Spain. We often go swimming in the summer.
Miu	Brilliant. I love swimming. But my sister and I ⁶ .... to a swimming pool! (go) We ⁷ .... in the sea. (not swim) It's very cold!
Pablo	What sports ⁸ .... you .... ? (do)
Miu	I ⁹ .... volleyball and ¹⁰ .... gymnastics. (play, do) ¹¹ .... you .... sport? (like)
Pablo	Yes, I ¹² .... I ¹³ .... football. (love) I always ¹⁴ .... Barcelona play on TV. (watch)
Miu	I ¹⁵ .... football. (not like) But my brother ¹⁶ .... for the school team. (play)
Pablo	Cool.

I mustn't use my mobile phone

1 Read the definitions and solve the anagrams.

ALRCOUCALT   LIPCEN ESCA   LURER   ECSREEXI OKOB   RASREE   RADOB

1 You use it in maths. _calculator_
2 You write in this. ....
3 You put your pens and
  pencils in this. ....

4 You correct your mistakes with it.
  ....
5 You draw lines with it. ....
6 Your teacher writes on this. ....

2 Complete the phrases with a verb. Sometimes use *don't*.

1 _Be_ .... quiet.
2 _Don't run_ .... in the corridor.
3 .... polite.
4 .... litter.
5 .... your mobile.

6 .... your school uniform.
7 .... your homework.
8 .... or drink in the classroom.
9 .... gum.
10 .... to music.

3 Match the expressions from Exercise 2 with the pictures.

A 5   B   C Please   D   E

F   G   H   I   J

39 Complete the conversations with the expressions. Then listen and check.

I'm not sure.   That's right.   I don't believe it!

1 **Owen** What time is it?
  Zoe   It's eight o'clock.
  Owen ....
          We're late for the film!

2 **Ella** What's the capital of China?
  Dan   It's Beijing.
  Ella ....

3 **Anthony** Is that girl's name Imogen?
  Peter   ....
             Let's ask her.

must – positive and negative

1 Complete the *house rules* with *must* (✓) or *mustn't* (✗).

1 You .... tidy your room.

2 You .... watch TV after nine o'clock.

3 You .... eat in your room.

4 You .... take the dog for a walk.

5 You .... help in the kitchen.

6 You .... go to bed late.

7 You .... do your homework.

8 You .... text your friends during dinner.

2 Complete the speech bubbles with *must* or *mustn't* and the verbs.

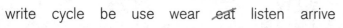

| write   cycle   be   use   wear   ~~eat~~   listen   arrive |

Suzy and Nick are always in trouble!

1 You must eat vegetables.

2 You .... school uniform.

3 You .... on the desk.

4 You .... your mobile.

5 You .... at nine o'clock.

6 You .... to music.

7 You .... in the playground!

8 You .... quiet in the exam.

3 Circle the correct word.

1 Who is that boy? **He** / **Him** is in my class.

2 I don't like dogs. Do you like **they** / **them**?

3 Where is Anna? I want to talk to **she** / **her**.

4 My brother and I like Manchester United. **We** / **Us** always go to their matches.

5 **A** Do you know that boy?
  B Yes, I sit next to **he** / **him** in class.

6 Nicole Kidman is a great actor. **She** / **Her** is very beautiful.

7 We're at the café. Can you join **we** / **us**?

8 Andy and Eddie are best friends. **They** / **Them** are always together.

9 I've got a new mp3 player. Do you want to see **him** / **it**?

10 You can have these pencils. I don't want **them** / **they**.

11 You're fun to be with! I like **us** / **you**.

4 Complete the sentences with the correct object pronoun.

1 These are my new trainers. Do you like them ?

2 No meat for me, please. I don't eat ....

3 The keys are on the table. Don't forget ....

4 This is my new mobile phone. Do you like ....?

5 Jessica isn't my friend. I don't like ....

6 Charlie is great fun. I like ....

7 Look! There are Lee's parents. Do you know ....?

8 This T-shirt is horrible. I don't want ....

9 We're late for the lesson. The teacher is very angry with ....

10 I like the new student and I think he likes ....!

Communication

1 ⊙ **40** Put the conversation in order. Then listen and check.

Jamie	I'm sorry, I can't. I'm busy. ☐
Olivia	Hi, Jamie. ☐ 1
Olivia	Oh, OK. Another time. ☐
Jamie	Hi, Olivia. ☐
Olivia	Would you like to come to the cinema? ☐

2 ⊙ **41** Complete the conversation. Then listen and check.

Tom	Hi, Lauren.
Lauren	Hi, Tom.
Tom	¹ .... you like to come to a party?
Lauren	A party?
Tom	Yes, it's my birthday party. Would you ² .... to come?
Lauren	Yes, I ³ .... When is it?
Tom	It's on Saturday at six o'clock. At Burger House.
Lauren	Brilliant! ⁴ .... you on Saturday.
Tom	Great.

Reading

Hi! My name's Daniel and I come from Germany. I'm 13. I like reading and animals. My favourite school subject is Music. I can play the piano. But I play the electric guitar, too, and I'm in a band! I like sport, too – I do judo. I speak German, English and a bit of French. I hope to get an email from you.

Hello. My name's Zeynep and I come from Turkey. I'm 11. I love films and books. My favourite school subjects are English and Turkish. I like animals. My favourite colour is red and my favourite animal is the elephant! I can speak Turkish, English and a bit of Arabic. My dream job is a zoo keeper! Contact me!

Hi! My name's James and I'm 12. I'm from Australia and I live in Melbourne. My favourite school subjects are History and Geography. My interests are music, playing computer games and taking photos. I play football and I'm a Soccaroos fan (that's our national team!). I speak English (obviously), and a bit of Chinese. My perfect penpal isn't English!

Hi, my name's Gaby and I'm from Mexico. I'm 12. I love parties, fashion, films and ... science. It's strange, I know, but my favourite school subject is Science. And my dream job is a scientist! I don't like sport. I hate football and tennis! I speak Spanish (Hola!) and English. Please be my penpal.

1 **Read about the students and (circle) the correct answers.**

1 Zeynep likes ...
   a music. **b** animals. **c** history.
2 Daniel ...
   a does judo. **b** doesn't like sport.
   c plays football.
3 James likes ...
   a playing the electric guitar. **b** playing the piano. **c** playing computer games.

4 Zeynep and Gaby like ...
   a elephants. **b** films. **c** science.
5 Daniel and James like ...
   a music. **b** history. **c** football.
6 Zeynep likes studying ...
   a Turkish. **b** Geography. **c** Science.
7 Daniel is ...
   a twelve. **b** eleven. **c** thirteen.
8 Gaby is from ...
   a Australia. **b** Germany. **c** Mexico.

Listening

2 ⊙ **42** **Listen to Tomasz and complete his email.**

| colour | United States | judo | films | eleven | actor | English | ~~Poland~~ | Maths | tennis |

Hi! I'm from **1** _Poland_ . I live with my family in Warsaw. My name's Tomasz and I'm **2** _____ . My favourite school subjects are **3** _____ and ICT. I love computer games and **4** _____ . I love sport, too, and I do **5** _____ and play **6** _____ . My dream job is an **7** _____ . My favourite **8** _____ is green. I speak Polish and **9** _____ . I want a penpal from the **10** _____ . Please write to me.

Writing

3 **Write to your *penpal*. Complete the text for you.**

Hi, my name's _____ and I'm from _____ . I live in _____ .
My favourite school subjects are _____ . I do/play/go _____ .
My interests are _____ . I love _____ . I don't like _____ .
I speak _____ . My dream job is _____ .

Your progress

Look at Student's Book Unit 6. Circle: ☺ **= not very well** ☺ **= quite well** ☺ **= very well**

I can read and understand school timetables.	☺ ☺ ☺	p69
I can talk about school subjects.	☺ ☺ ☺	p69
I can talk about school rules.	☺ ☺ ☺	p73
I can listen and understand a person talking about their life.	☺ ☺ ☺	p76
I can read a notice board and understand the notices.	☺ ☺ ☺	p77
I can write an email describing my school and school day.	☺ ☺ ☺	p77
I can invite friends to a party and write simple invitations.	☺ ☺ ☺	p123

Your project: personal rules!

• Write five things you *must* do and five things you *mustn't* do. For example:
  I must put my litter in the bin. I mustn't eat lots of sweets.
• Make a rules poster. Draw pictures.
• Put the list on your bedroom wall.
  Try to memorise the rules.

My personal rules

I must be nice to my little brother.

I mustn't watch TV all day.

1 Complete the crossword.

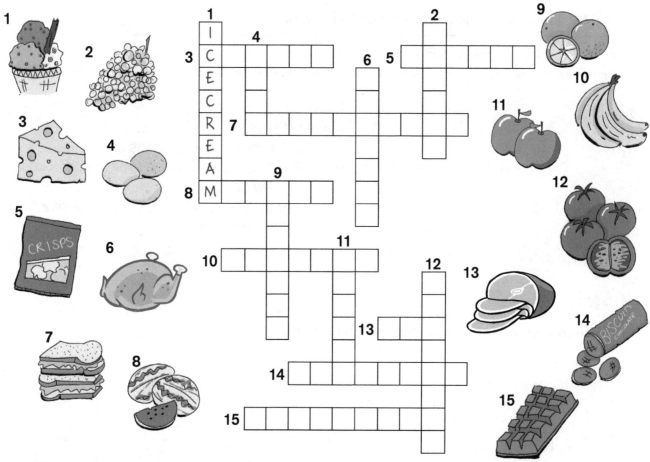

2 Write words from the crossword for you.

I often eat	I sometimes eat	I never eat

Chat zone

🔊 **43 Complete the conversations with the expressions. Then listen and check.**

Let's go!   Wait a minute!   Only joking.

1 Maya We've got an English exam tomorrow!
Amy Oh no! That's terrible!
Maya ....

2 Sam Have you got your mobile phone? And your money?
Dan Yes, I have.
Sam OK. ....
        We're late.

3 Mum Come on, Alex. It's time to go to school!
Alex ....
        I can't find my pencil case.

Countable and uncountable nouns

1 Look at the pictures and complete the words with the missing vowels.

1 ...... p p l ......

2 p ...... p ...... r

3 c ...... l ......

4 p h ...... n ......

5 c ...... m p ...... t ...... r

6 c h ...... l d

7 w ...... t ...... r

8 s h ......

9 p ...... n c l

10 m ...... n ...... y

11 b .... k

12 m ...... s c

13 w ...... m ...... n

14 h ...... r

15 h ...... m ...... w ...... r k

16 i n f ...... r m ...... t ...... n

2 Complete the spidergrams with the words from Exercise 1.

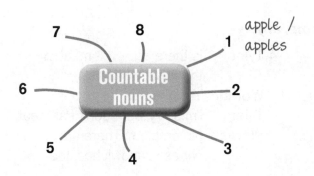

Countable nouns

1 apple / apples
2
3
4
5
6
7
8

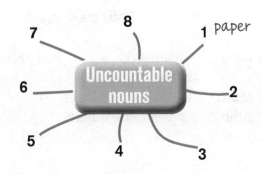

Uncountable nouns

1 paper
2
3
4
5
6
7
8

3 (Circle) the correct words.

1 There is **a** / (some) cheese.
2 There aren't **some** / **any** computers.
3 Is there **a** / **any** phone?
4 There isn't **a** / **any** money.
5 There are **some** / **any** pens.
6 Are there **a** / **any** postcards?
7 There are **some** / **any** comics.
8 There is **a** / **some** water.
9 There is **an** / **any** egg.
10 There isn't **some** / **any** fruit.

4 Put the words in the correct order.

1 crisps / any / there / are ?
   Are there any crisps?

2 any / bag / my / isn't / there / in / chocolate
3 are / some / grapes / there
4 in / any / fridge / are / tomatoes / there / the / ?
5 aren't / bananas / any / there
6 the / there / desk / are / on / some / books
7 any / isn't / there / cola
8 an / today / is / lesson / there / English / ?

5 **What's in the fridge? Complete the questions and write short answers.**

1 water   Is there any water?
             Yes, there is.

2 eggs   Are there any eggs?
             No, there aren't.

3 bananas   ....

4 chicken   ....

5 tomatoes   ....

6 fish   ....

7 cheese   ....

8 oranges   ....

9 cola   ....

10 apples   ....

6 **Complete the conversations with *a*, *an*, *some*, *any*.**

1 Joe   Have you got ...any........ chocolate?

Alex   No, I haven't. But I've got .... apple.

Joe   I don't like fruit.

2 Daisy   Is there .... good music on your mp3 player?

George   Yes, there is! Listen. This is .... good song.

3 Lara   I haven't got .... money.

Harriet   Oh dear.

Lara   Have you got .... money?

Harriet   No, I haven't.

4 Tyler   Is there .... meat in these sandwiches?

Woman   Yes, there is.

Tyler   I'm sorry, but I don't eat meat.

Woman   No problem. There are .... cheese sandwiches, too.

5 Leo   Are there .... computers in your school?

Erin   Yes, there are. And there are .... DVD players, too.

6 Alfie   There isn't .... fruit juice in the fridge.

Mum   Drink .... water.

Alfie   I never drink water!

1 (Circle) 12 food and drink words.

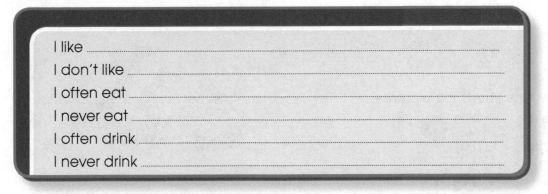

carrots teapotatoeslambstrawberriesmilkbeefpeaspearsnutsorangesturkey

2 Write sentences about food for you.

I like ....
I don't like ....
I often eat ....
I never eat ....
I often drink ....
I never drink ....

3 ⊙ 44 Match the questions with the answers. Then listen and check.

1 How many crisps do you eat a week?

2 How much meat do you eat?

3 How much milk do you drink a week?

4 How much fish do you eat?

5 How many oranges do you eat?

6 How much cola do you drink?

a None. I don't like cola!

b Not many. I usually eat apples.

c Not a lot. I only have it in coffee and with my breakfast cereal.

d None. I don't eat it. I'm a vegetarian.

e A lot. I eat a packet every day!

f Quite a lot. I always eat it on Friday with chips!

4 Answer the questions from Exercise 3 for you.

1 ....
2 ....
3 ....
4 ....
5 ....
6 ....

much / many / lots

1 Complete the questions with *How much* or *How many.*

1 _How many_ cousins have you got?
2 _____ milk is in the fridge?
3 _____ cakes are there?
4 _____ emails do you write a week?
5 _____ rooms are in your home?
6 _____ ice cream is there?
7 _____ books do you read a year?
8 _____ rice do you want?

2 Write questions about the pictures.

1

How many women are there?

2

How much cheese is there?

3

_____

4

_____

5

_____

6

_____

3 Write questions for these answers. Use *How much ...?* or *How many ...?*

1 How many books are there?
  There are ten books.
2 How much pasta do you eat?
  I eat lots of pasta.
3 _____
  I don't drink any milk.
4 _____
  There are 20 students in my class.
5 _____
  I listen to lots of music.
6 _____
  I send about ten text messages a day.
7 _____
  I don't buy many sweets.
8 _____
  I watch lots of films.

4 ⌾Circle the correct words.

1 There aren't **much** / **many** sandwiches.
2 We eat **lots of** / **much** vegetables.
3 There is **lots of** / **much** rice.
4 I haven't got **much** / **many** comics.
5 There isn't **much** / **many** sugar.
6 My dad hasn't got **much** / **many** DVDs.

5 Complete the sentences with *There is/are* and *lots of*, *not much* or *not many*.

1
There is lots of luggage.

2
There aren't many people.

3
.... cars.

4
.... water.

5
.... chips.

6
.... cakes.

7
.... lemonade.

8
.... postcards.

Communication

🔊 **45** Complete the conversations. Then listen and check.

like	would	anything	here	have

A School cook　Hello. What ¹ .... you like?
Ethan　　　Can I ² .... a jacket potato with cheese, please?
School cook　³ .... else?
Ethan　　　I'd ⁴ .... some ice cream, please.
School cook　⁵ .... you are.
Ethan　　　Thanks.

no	thank	can	what	like

B School cook　Hello. ⁶ .... would you like?
Jade　　　　Have you got any chicken?
School cook　Yes, we've got chicken curry.
Jade　　　　Mmm. ⁷ .... I have chicken curry, please?
School cook　Yes, of course. Would you ⁸ .... a dessert?
Jade　　　　⁹ .... , thanks.
School cook　OK. Here's your curry.
Jade　　　　¹⁰ .... you.

Reading

1 Find this information in the article.

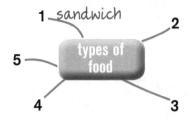

1 sandwich
2
5
types of food
4
3

1 energy
2
things you get from food
3

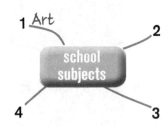

1 Art
2
school subjects
4
3

2 Read the article and complete the sentences with numbers.

1 .... people around the world go to bed hungry.

2 .... children die of hunger every day.

3 The WFP gives food to .... people.

4 You give .... rice grains when you get a correct answer in the 'Free rice' game.

5 About .... people play the 'Free rice' game every day.

From hunger to hope

1 Are you hungry? How about a sandwich or some fruit? Or is it dinnertime? What about a nice steak, or some chicken and rice? But imagine – lots of people around the world don't have regular meals. And dinner is just a small plate of food. Do you know 850 million people around the world go to bed hungry?

2 Food gives you energy, and it also gives you important vitamins and minerals. Without good food children don't grow and get sick. 10,000 children around the world die every day because they haven't got much food.

3 The United Nations World Food Program (WFP) gives food to poor people around the world. It helps when there are terrible disasters or when there is no rain. It gives food to about 90 million people a year, including 58 million children. Sometimes it gives lunch to children at school.

4 How can you help? You can go to the UN website and play the 'Free rice' game. There are quizzes about vocabulary, Art, Maths, Science and Geography. Every time you get a correct answer you give 20 rice grains to the WFP. Students and teachers around the world love the quizzes, and about 40,000 people play every day. So, how much rice is that?

3 Read the article again. Match the words with the definitions.

Paragraph 1 (you want food) (poor)

(you put food on this) (sick)

Paragraph 2 (not well) (grains)

Paragraph 3 (not rich) (plate)

Paragraph 4 (small pieces of rice) (hungry)

Listening

4 ◉ **46** **Listen to the students and complete what they say.**

Thomas I have ¹ .... and cereal for breakfast. At lunchtime I have ² .... , an apple and some cake. I usually have meat and ³ .... for dinner. But I don't like beef. I sometimes have ice cream, too.

Olivia I have ⁴ .... , bread and cheese for breakfast. I have lunch at school. I often eat crisps. My favourite meal at school is tomato ⁵ .... In the evenings we often have ⁶ .... curry or chicken and rice.

Chloe I have milk and fruit for breakfast. I have a big lunch. I eat ⁷ .... and vegetables. My favourite meal is ⁸ .... and chips. But I don't have it very often.

Writing

5 **Write a paragraph about your diet. Use the sentences below to help you.**

- I have .... for breakfast / lunch / dinner.
- I have / eat / drink ....
- I usually have .... for dinner.
- I don't have .... very often.
- My favourite food is ....
- I love / don't like ....

I have ....

Your progress

Look at Student's Book Unit 7. Circle: ☹ = not very well ☺ = quite well 😄 = very well

I can talk about quantities and plan a picnic.	☹ ☺ 😄	p79
I can ask and answer questions using *is there* and *are there*.	☹ ☺ 😄	p81
I can read and understand a questionnaire.	☹ ☺ 😄	p83
I can write about my favourite food.	☹ ☺ 😄	p83
I can listen and identify food on trays.	☹ ☺ 😄	p86
I can write a food diary.	☹ ☺ 😄	p86
I can order food and drink in a school canteen.	☹ ☺ 😄	p124

Your project: memory game

- Make 24 cards. Decorate the back of each one with a smiley ☺.
- On 12 cards write the names of food, for example: *apple, fish, cake*
- On the other 12 cards draw pictures of the same words.
- Put all the cards down on the table, smiley ☺ side up.
- Try to match words and pictures. Turn one card. Then turn another card. Are they the same? If yes, leave them. If not, put them back.
- Try again until you find all the pairs.

1 Write the names of the animals.

1 _elephant_   2 _____   3 _____   4 _____

5 _____   6 _____   7 _____   8 _____

2 Write the names of the animals.

gorilla   ~~ostrich~~   snake   snail   whale   parrot

1

ostrich

2

_____

3

_____

4

_____

5

_____

6

_____

3 Put the animals in groups. Animals can go in more than one group.

WHICH ANIMALS CAN …

1 climb trees? _____

2 you ride? _____

3 eat plants and leaves? _____

4 eat meat? _____

5 speak? _____

6 swim? _____

7 fly? _____

4 🔘 **47** Complete the text messages with the words. Then listen and check.

horses   sister   city   opposite   brilliant   ~~parents~~   message   garden

I'm having a day out in London with my ¹ _parents_ and it's fantastic. We're standing in the London Eye. It's ² _____
the Houses of Parliament. We're high up. And we're looking at Big Ben and the River Thames. I can see all of the ³ _____ !
Alicia

Hi! I'm sending this ⁴ _____ from Warwick Castle. The castle is ⁵ _____ . I'm watching knights on ⁶ _____ .
They're so cool! I'm sitting next to my dad. But my mum and ⁷ _____ aren't watching the knights. They're visiting the ⁸ _____ . Boring!
Hamed

Present continuous – positive

1 Look at the pictures and complete the text message.

| having | eating | looking at | drawing | buying | ~~visiting~~ |

Hi! We're ..*visiting*.. the zoo. It's great! I'm ¹.......................... the kangaroos. My brother Jason is ².......................... a picture of a bear. My parents are ³.......................... ice cream. The elephants are ⁴.......................... a shower. The bear is ⁵.......................... an apple.

2 Complete the sentences with the present continuous.

1 I .*'m doing*... my homework. (do)
2 My team .*is winning*. the match. (win)
3 We .... our dinner. (eat)
4 They .... to school. (walk)

5 The children .... in the classroom. (sit)
6 My dad .... cakes. (make)
7 He .... in the sea. (swim)
8 The tourist .... photos. (take)

3 Look at the pictures and write sentences.

1  They .*'re dancing*..

2  James and Charlie .... a race.

3  She .... the guitar.

4  They .... a song.

5  Clare .... a bus.

6  They .... on the phone.

7  My mum .... computer games.

8  I .... a bike.

4 Write sentences in the negative form.

1 We're eating lunch.
  We aren't eating lunch.
2 They're playing tennis.

3 She's having breakfast.

4 I'm studying for a test.

5 My brother is taking a photo.

6 The gorillas are climbing the tree.

5 Write sentences. Use the short forms.

1  he / work
  He isn't working.
  He's sleeping.

2  you / read

3  we / listen to music

4  Paul / walk

5  they / send
  text messages

6  she / drive a car

Prepositions of place

6 Look at the picture and circle the prepositions.

1 The giraffe is **in front of / opposite** the monkeys.
2 The lions are **next to / behind** the elephants.
3 The kangaroos are **behind / opposite** the giraffe.
4 The koala bears are **opposite / in front of** the lions.
5 The bears are **in front of / next to** the lions.
6 The ice cream van is **in front of / behind** the entrance.
7 The tortoises are **next to / opposite** the tigers.
8 The ticket office is **in front of / next to** the café.

1 Describe the weather.

It's cloudy.   It's windy.   ~~It's sunny.~~   It's raining.   It's foggy.   It's snowing.

1 It's sunny. **2** .... **3** .... **4** .... **5** .... **6** ....

2 Write a list of the clothes you wear:

1 When it's hot and sunny.

....

2 When it's snowing.

....

3 When it's raining.

....

trainers   skirt
shirt   dress
trousers   T-shirt
tie   sweater
jacket   coat
shoes   shorts

3 Complete the conversation for you.

You	Hi! Where are you calling from?
Your friend	I'm in ¹ .... ! What's the weather like at home?
You	It's ² .... It's great!
Your friend	It's ³ .... here. It's terrible!
You	Are you having a good time?

Your friend	⁴ ....
You	What are you doing?
Your friend	I'm talking to you and I'm eating a ⁵ ....
You	What's your mum doing?
Your friend	She's ⁶ ....
You	What's your brother doing?
Your friend	He's ⁷ ....
You	That's great! See you soon.

Chat zone

◉ 48 Complete the conversations with the expressions. Then listen and check.

Poor you!   It's the best thing ever!   Help!

1 Leo I've got lots of homework!
  Erin ....

2 Dan There's a snake in my room!
  ....

3 Lisa Do you like your new computer game?
  Tom ....

Present continuous – questions and short answers

1 Write questions and answers.

he / ride / a horse?

1 Is he riding a horse?
No, he isn't.

she / listen / to music?

2 Is she listening to music?
Yes, she is.

she / write / a letter?

3 ....
....

you / draw / an elephant?

4 ....
....

they / wear / T-shirts?

5 ....
....

he / eat / a pizza?

6 ....
....

2 Complete the phone conversations.

1 A What _are_ .... you
doing .... (do)?
B I _'m eating_ .... a sandwich (eat).

2 A Where are you?
B I .... on a bus (sit).
Are you at home?
A No, I .... (not).
I .... a bike race (watch).

3 A What .... you .... (do)?
B I .... a new computer game (play).
A Lucky you. I .... games (not play).
I .... my room (tidy)!

4 A .... Alice and Emma
.... lunch (make)?
B No, they .... (not). They ....
to music in the sitting room (listen).

Present continuous or present simple?

3 ⟨Circle⟩ the correct words.
1 I **play** / **am playing** football every Tuesday and Thursday.
2 We usually **walk** / **are walking** to school.
3 They **have** / **are having** lunch at the moment.
4 Faruk **stands** / **is standing** in front of Buckingham Palace.
5 Where **do you go** / **are you going** ?
6 I never **read** / **am reading** a school book in bed.
7 I **go** / **am going** to bed late at the weekend.
8 Look! Juan **talks** / **is talking** to Alicia.

4 Look at the pictures and complete the sentences.

Tim's tropical holiday ✦

1  Tim usually _sits_ in a classroom. Today he _'s sitting_ on the beach.

2  He usually .... coffee and biscuits for breakfast. Today he .... two bananas and a melon!

3  He usually .... in a swimming pool. Today he .... in the sea.

4  Tim and his sister, Eve, usually .... computer games. Today they .... volleyball on the beach.

5  Eve usually .... school books. Today she .... magazines.

6  Tim usually .... to bed early. Today he .... to bed late.

Communication

◉ **49** The tourists are in the Tourist Information Centre (TIC). Look at the map and complete the conversations. Then listen and check.

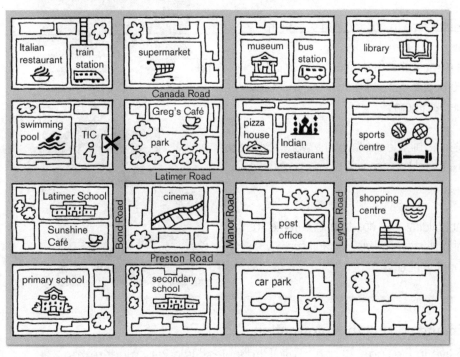

A Tourist ¹ .... me, where's the secondary school?

Woman Go right. Go straight on. Take the second ² .... It's on the ³ .... in Preston Road.

Tourist ⁴ .... you very much.

Woman You're welcome.

B Tourist Excuse me, where's the shopping centre?

Woman Go ⁵ .... Then turn ⁶ .... Take the ⁷ .... right. It's on Leyton Road.

Tourist Thank you very much.

Woman ⁸ .... welcome.

Reading

1 Read the web page and match the pictures with the paragraphs.

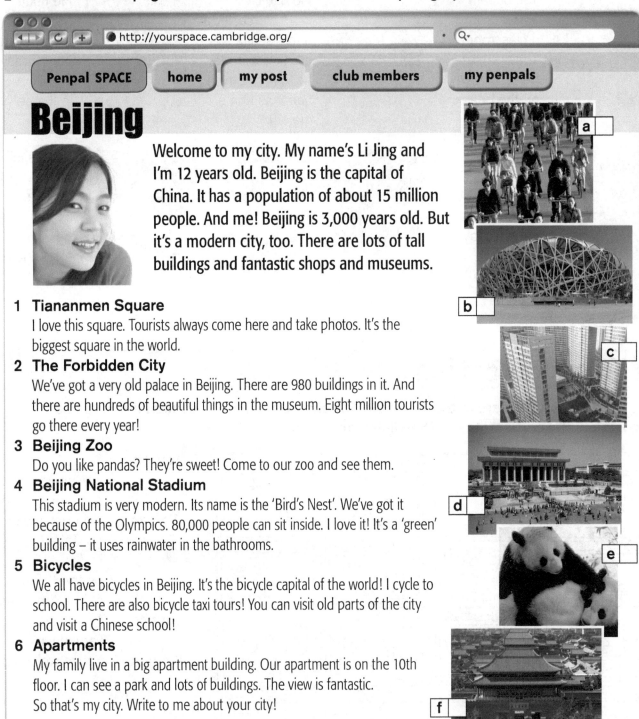

http://yourspace.cambridge.org/

Penpal SPACE | home | my post | club members | my penpals

Beijing

Welcome to my city. My name's Li Jing and I'm 12 years old. Beijing is the capital of China. It has a population of about 15 million people. And me! Beijing is 3,000 years old. But it's a modern city, too. There are lots of tall buildings and fantastic shops and museums.

1 Tiananmen Square
I love this square. Tourists always come here and take photos. It's the biggest square in the world.

2 The Forbidden City
We've got a very old palace in Beijing. There are 980 buildings in it. And there are hundreds of beautiful things in the museum. Eight million tourists go there every year!

3 Beijing Zoo
Do you like pandas? They're sweet! Come to our zoo and see them.

4 Beijing National Stadium
This stadium is very modern. Its name is the 'Bird's Nest'. We've got it because of the Olympics. 80,000 people can sit inside. I love it! It's a 'green' building – it uses rainwater in the bathrooms.

5 Bicycles
We all have bicycles in Beijing. It's the bicycle capital of the world! I cycle to school. There are also bicycle taxi tours! You can visit old parts of the city and visit a Chinese school!

6 Apartments
My family live in a big apartment building. Our apartment is on the 10th floor. I can see a park and lots of buildings. The view is fantastic. So that's my city. Write to me about your city!

a
b
c
d
e
f

2 Read the web page again and correct the information.

1 About ~~10~~ million people live in Beijing. ..15..
2 Beijing is about 2,000 years old.
3 Lots of tourists go to Tiananmen Square and draw pictures.
4 There are 980 museums in the Forbidden City.
5 The 'Bird's Nest' is a very modern zoo.
6 80,000 people can stand in the National Stadium.
7 Beijing is the taxi capital of the world.
8 Li's apartment is on the twelfth floor of an apartment building.

Listening

3 ◉ **50** **Where are the students? Listen and match the cities with the names.**

Alfie (1)   Lauren (2)   Sam (3)   Zoe (4)

4 ◉ **50** **Listen again and circle.**

1 Alfie says the taxis are **yellow / black**.
2 He **loves / doesn't like** the Statue of Liberty.
3 Lauren says about **15 / 50** million people live in Mexico City.
4 She says they speak **French / Spanish**.
5 Sam is staying in **a hotel / a house**.

6 His favourite thing is **Big Ben / the black taxis**.
7 Zoe says the Colosseum is a famous ancient **museum / stadium**.
8 Her favourite thing is **ice cream / pizza**.

Writing

5 **Write to Li Jing about your two favourite cities.**

Name of place

What it is

Why I like it

Name of place

What it is

Why I like it

Your progress

Look at Student's Book Unit 8. Circle: ☹ = not very well ☺ = quite well 😄 = very well

I can read short text messages and understand the meaning.	☹ ☺ 😄	p89
I can talk about actions in progress.	☹ ☺ 😄	p89 & p92
I can talk about the weather.	☹ ☺ 😄	p92
I can read and understand information about a city.	☹ ☺ 😄	p96
I can listen and understand where a person is.	☹ ☺ 😄	p96
I can write a short description of a town.	☹ ☺ 😄	p96
I can ask the way, give and read directions.	☹ ☺ 😄	p125

Your project: holiday blog

- Imagine you are on holiday. Decide:
  where you are   where you are staying
  what you are doing   the weather   how you feel
- Now write an imaginary blog about your holiday every day for a week.
- Use the present continuous. For example:
  It's Saturday. I'm walking in the mountains. I'm with my father. It's snowing and it's cold. I'm tired. I'm not happy!
- Then present your blog to the class.

1 Complete the crossword.

1 GR8
2 LUV
3 L8R
4 2MORO
5 HOW R U?
6 2
7 C U
8 2DAY

2 Fill in the text messages with the correct abbreviations.

1
Hi, Jo, ...? (how are you)
Matt

2
.................! (great)
Jo

3
.... at home? (are you)
Matt

4
Yes. How about ....? (you)
Jo

5
I'm in the supermarket.
Matt

6
OK! .... (see you later)
Jo

7
Yes, ... (see you tomorrow)
Matt

Chat zone

🔘 **51** Complete the conversations with the expressions. Then listen and check.

Boring!   Get well soon.   Hi guys.

1 Imogen Hi, Mark. How are you?
Mark I feel horrible. I was in bed all day yesterday.
Imogen Poor you. ....
Mark Thanks.

2 Laura ....
Anna Hi, Laura.
Kate Where were you this morning?
Laura I was at home with my mum.

3 Sophie What are you watching on TV?
Adam Rugby.
Sophie ....

Past simple verb *be* – positive

1 (Circle) the correct form of *be*. Then match the pictures to the sentences.

1 It **was** / **were** my sister's birthday yesterday. [g]
2 We **were** / **was** at school on Wednesday. ☐
3 Grace **was** / **were** on the phone last night. ☐
4 They **was** / **were** in London last week. ☐
5 He **were** / **was** at the shops all day. ☐
6 I **was** / **were** in the garden at 10.00 am this morning. ☐
7 You **were** / **was** tired after swimming. ☐
8 Jade and Luke **were** / **was** in Paris two days ago. ☐

a

b
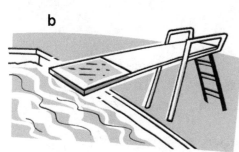

c

d
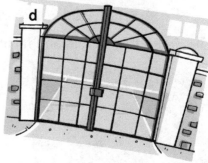

e

f

g

h

2 Look at Sarah's diary for last week and finish the sentences.

Monday	Friday
Dad – Sports Centre	Disco
Tuesday	**Saturday**
My birthday!	Shops with Megan
Wednesday	**Sunday**
Mum and Kim – Manchester	Megan's house
Thursday	
Sunny!	

1 On Monday Dad __was__ at the __sports__ __centre__ .
2 Last _____ it _____ my birthday.
3 Mum and Kim _____ in _____ on Wednesday.
4 On _____ it _____ sunny.
5 I _____ at the disco on _____ .
6 On _____ Megan and I _____ at the shops.
7 I _____ at _____ on Sunday.

Past simple verb *be* – negative

3 **Make the sentences negative.**

1 I was at school yesterday.
I wasn't at school yesterday.

2 Last night he was tired.
....

3 They were in Paris a week ago.
....

4 In 2008 you were at primary school.
....

5 We were at the swimming pool this morning.
....

6 On Thursday she was at home.
....

7 It was cold yesterday.
....

8 Nick and Joe were on holiday last month.
....

Past simple *be* – questions and short answers

4 **Read the factfile and fill in the gaps.**

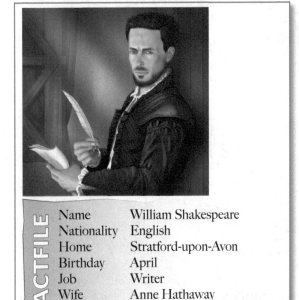

FACTFILE	
Name	William Shakespeare
Nationality	English
Home	Stratford-upon-Avon
Birthday	April
Job	Writer
Wife	Anne Hathaway
Children	Susanna, Hamnet and Judith

1 *Was* Shakespeare's first name Bob?
No, it wasn't, it was *William* .

2 .... his birthday in ....?
Yes, ...

3 .... he Scottish?
...................., he wasn't. .... English.

4 .... his home in London?
No, ... It was ....

5 .... his children's names Susanna, Hamnet and Judith?
...................., they ....

6 .... he a scientist?
No, ... He ....

7 .... his wife's name Anne Hathaway?
...................., it ....

5 **Write the questions and short answers.**

1 Christopher Columbus / British / ?
No / Italian
Was Christopher Columbus British?
No, he wasn't. He was Italian.

2 The Beatles / from Germany / ?
No / England
....

3 Ayrton Senna / a racing driver / ?
Yes
....

4 Picasso and Dali / Mexican / ?
No / Spanish
....

5 Einstein / a dentist / ?
No / a scientist
....

6 Mary Shelley / a writer / ?
Yes
....

7 Beethoven and Mozart / composers / ?
Yes
....

8 Marie Curie / from France / ?
No / from Poland
....

1 Circle ten vehicles.

motorbiketrainspaceshipcaryachtbicycleshiphelicopterbusplane

2 Label the vehicles in the picture.

1	2	3	4	5

6	7	8	9	10

Past simple positive – regular verbs

1 **Complete the sentences with one of these verbs in the past simple.**

arrive   play   start   sail   film   ~~decide~~   juggle   cook   study

1 He _decided_ to go by bike to the sports centre after school.

2 We were very hungry last night so we .... pizza.

3 He .... football all day in the park yesterday.

4 Last Friday they .... seven balls at the school show.

5 Six months ago she .... around the world on her own.

6 Last weekend you .... for your exams.

7 Jack and Lucy .... early at George's house.

8 The teacher .... the school show with his new camera.

9 She .... her journey at six o'clock in the morning.

Common regular verbs

2 **Complete the sentences with these verbs in the past simple.**

phone   like   wash   dance   ~~live~~   carry   talk   paint

1 I _lived_ in London ten years ago.
2 David .... milk when he was little.
3 Last night you .... to your friend for hours!
4 We .... nice pictures at school yesterday.

5 Last week Sara .... her grandparents every day.
6 When they were teenagers, my parents .... at the disco every weekend!
7 This morning she .... the shopping for her mum at the supermarket.
8 When I was young, I .... my hair every evening.

3 Look at the table and write about the friends and their weekend.

	Ruby	Jonny
Saturday morning	listen to music	surf the web
Saturday afternoon	call Jonny	talk to Ruby
Saturday evening	visit grandparents	study
Sunday morning	watch TV	cook a meal
Sunday afternoon	help parents in the home	play computer games
Sunday evening	work	do homework

1 On Saturday evening, Jonny _studied_ and Ruby _visited_ her _grandparents_ .
2 On Sunday afternoon, Ruby .... her ....
3 On Sunday morning, Jonny .... and Ruby ....
4 Ruby .... on Saturday morning.
5 On Saturday afternoon, Ruby .... Jonny.
6 Jonny .... on Saturday morning and in the afternoon he ....
7 Jonny .... on Sunday afternoon.
8 On Sunday evening, Ruby .... and Jonny ....

Communication

1 Look at the bus timetable and answer the questions.

1 Where does the
  bus go? ....
2 How much is an adult
  single ticket? ....
3 How much is a child
  return ticket? ....
4 Where do you buy
  tickets? ....

"TO CAMBRIDGE CITY CENTRE"

BUY TICKETS ON THE BUS

Adult single £1.30

Adult return £2.20

Child single £0.80

Child return £1.40

2 🔘 **52** Complete the conversation. Then listen and check.

Ali	Does this bus go to the city [1] .... ?
Bus driver	Yes, it does.
Ali	[2] .... , please.
Bus driver	[3] .... fare?
Ali	Yes, please.
Bus driver	That's £[4] .... please.
Ali	Here you [5] ....
Bus driver	Thanks.
Ali	Thank you. Oh, can you tell me where to [6] .... , please?
Bus driver	OK!

Reading

1 **Read the blogs and match the names with the questions.**

1 Who danced for hours at a disco?   Rocky
2 Who played football in the park?   Sophie
3 Who studied all weekend?   Emily

By: Emily   Mood: ☺   Date: September 21st

Hi there! My weekend was busy but fun! I stayed at my friend's house on Saturday night and we watched a film. On Sunday we played football in the park with my friend's brother. Back to school tomorrow. Bye!

By: Rocky   Mood: ☹   Date: September 21st

My weekend wasn't very interesting … I studied all day Saturday and all day Sunday. I've got an exam on Monday. My mum cooked nice meals for me but I was still bored. I missed my friends! See you.

By: Sophie   Mood: 😐   Date: September 22nd

I'm so tired! On Saturday I visited my grandparents and sailed on their yacht. Then on Saturday evening I danced for hours at a disco with my friends. All day Sunday I helped my parents in the house – I tidied my room. I'm going to bed. Goodnight!

2 **Decide if the sentences are true (*T*) or false (*F*).**

1 Sophie visited her friends and sailed in their yacht. _F_
2 Emily was happy about her weekend. ....
3 Rocky's weekend was very interesting. ....
4 Emily watched a film with her friend on Saturday night. ....
5 On Saturday Sophie helped her parents in the house. ....
6 Rocky cooked nice meals for his mum. ....

3 **Now rewrite the false sentences so they are true.**

1 Sophie visited her grandparents and sailed in their yacht.

Listening

4 **53** **Listen and write a tick (✓) or a cross (✗) in the table.**

	Sahara	Ben	Tomasz
visited Manchester	✓	✗	✓
stayed at home			
talked to grandparents			
talked on the phone			
watched TV			
enjoyed yesterday			

Writing

5 **Write four sentences about yesterday for you. Use the verbs to help you.**

> listen to music   phone a friend   ~~visit grandparents~~   study   play basketball
> ~~watch TV~~   enjoy yesterday   play computer games   cook a meal   wash hair

I watched TV in the evening.   I didn't visit my grandparents.

Your progress

Look at Student's Book Unit 9. Circle: ☹ = not very well ☺ = quite well 😄 = very well

I can talk about and understand where people were.	☹ ☺ 😄	p89
I can write simple sentences about the past.	☹ ☺ 😄	p101
I can ask and answer about feelings.	☹ ☺ 😄	p101
I can read an article about travellers and understand the information.	☹ ☺ 😄	p106
I can listen and understand information about historical events.	☹ ☺ 😄	p107
I can buy train and bus tickets.	☹ ☺ 😄	p126

Your project: a famous person

- Prepare a presentation. You can use a computer if you want.
- Choose someone famous from the past. Find information and pictures:

Basic information: his/her name birthday nationality

Home life: his/her home town job children

Life events: what he/she did why he/she is famous when he/she died

- Give your presentation to the class. Start in this way:

This is my presentation about Charlie Chaplin. He was a famous actor.
Finish with your opinion:

I like Charlie Chaplin because he was very funny. Thank you for listening.

1 **Complete Harry's weekend plans.**

Saturday 11 am

1 stay ....

Saturday 12.30

2 go ....

Saturday 2 pm

3 go ....

Saturday 4 pm

4 play ....

Saturday 7 pm

5 watch ....

Sunday 1 pm

6 have ....

Sunday 4 pm

7 play ....

Sunday 6 pm

8 tidy ....

Sunday 9 pm

9 do ....

2 **Match the verbs and nouns.**

1 stay
2 tidy
3 go
4 play
5 watch
6 go to
7 have

a the skate park
b your desk
c at home
d running
e lunch
f the guitar
g a film

Chat zone

🔘 **54** **Complete the conversations with the expressions. Then listen and check.**

| I'm not sure.   Go on!   It sounds fun. |

1 **Elliot** Do you want to play football this afternoon?
David What time?
Elliot At about three o'clock?
David I feel a bit tired.
Elliot ....
David OK then. See you in the park at three!

2 **Esme** What are you doing on Saturday?
Keira We're going to the Science Museum in the morning. Then in the afternoon we're going to the cinema.
Esme ....
Keira What are you doing?
Esme .... I haven't got any plans.

Present continuous for future arrangements

1 **Write the correct verb in the sentences.**

go to   go   ~~watch~~   play   stay   tidy

1

I 's watching
TV this evening.

2

They _____
at home on Sunday.

3

She _____
her room in the morning.

4

We _____
football tomorrow.

5

You _____
the museum next Friday.

6

He _____
shopping with Jade this
afternoon.

2 **Complete the conversation using the verbs.**

Mum   Are you doing your homework this
afternoon, Billy? (do)

Billy   Yes, I am!

Mum   _____ you _____ your
room this morning? (tidy)

Billy   No, I'm not. I 'm _____ in bed this
morning. (stay)

Mum   Oh no, you're not! It's ten o'clock!

Billy   Is it? I _____ swimming with
Chris in half an hour! (go)

Mum   What?

Billy   Yeah! And at two o'clock we _____ tennis. (play) And at five o'clock we
_____ to the cinema. (go) After that we _____ dinner (have) and at
nine o'clock we _____ TV. (watch)

Mum   So what time _____ you _____ your homework? (do)

Billy   I'm not sure …

Mum   You _____ at home today, Billy! (stay)

3 Look at the information and complete the conversation.

Time	Sasha's school trip	Jamie's school trip
9.30 am	leave school	leave school
10.30 am	go to the theatre	visit the museum
12.00 pm	eat lunch in a restaurant	have a picnic in the park
2.00 pm	meet the actors in the theatre	do homework in the museum
4.00 pm	go home	go back to school

Sasha What time are you leaving school tomorrow?
Jamie I'm leaving school at 9.30 am
Sasha Me too! Are you going to the theatre?
Jamie No, I'm not. I' ....
Sasha At 12.00 I'm eating lunch in a restaurant. What are you doing?
Jamie I' ....
Sasha But it's winter! What are you doing at 2.00 pm?
Jamie ....
Sasha Poor you! I'm meeting the actors! I'm going home at 4.00 pm. What about you?
Jamie ....!
Sasha Boring!

Prepositions of time

4 Match the words with the prepositions.

> ~~six o'clock~~ Wednesday the morning 7ᵗʰ January midnight
> the weekend Sunday March lunchtime 2002 my birthday

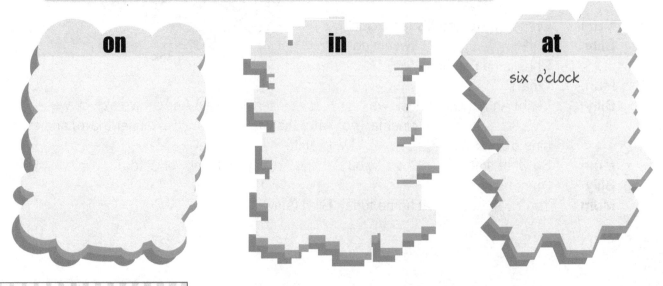

on

in

at

six o'clock

1 🔘 **55** Read the quiz and circle the correct answers. Then listen and check.

THE SECOND AMAZING QUIZ

1 .... can't jump.
a horses
b tigers
c elephants

2 An American football team has got ...
a 11 players.
b 12 players.
c 15 players.

3 What is she doing?
a She's skiing.
b She's surfing.
c She's skating.

4 Where is this bridge?
a London
b San Francisco
c Tokyo

5 The Olympic Games happen every ...
a two years.
b four years.
c five years.

6 A text message is an sms. What does sms mean?
a Speaking Message Service
b Short Message Service
c Silent Message Service

7 Julius Caesar was an ...
a ancient Greek.
b ancient Egyptian.
c ancient Roman.

8 .... invented the World Wide Web in 1994.
a Albert Einstein
b Tim Berners-Lee
c Bill Gates

9 Which of these animals lives in Antarctica?
a reindeer
b polar bears
c penguins

10 Which city was Marco Polo from?
a Venice
b Madrid
c Beijing

11 In very hot weather, you ...
a must eat lots of ice cream.
b mustn't wear white clothes.
c must drink lots of water.

12 The Aztecs lived in ...
a Mexico.
b India.
c China.

Talking about possessions

1   Look at the factfile about Keiko. Write the words in the correct order to make questions. Then write short answers.

FACTFILE

Keiko Mackenzie

Age:	12
Lives:	London
Hair:	black
Eyes:	brown
Family:	mum, dad, 1 sister
Pets:	2 cats, 1 dog
Mobile phone:	yes
TV in bedroom:	no
Garden:	yes

1   brown hair / has / got / Keiko?
    Has Keiko got brown hair?
    No, she hasn't.

2   got / she / eyes / brown / has?
    ....

3   any / Keiko / has / brothers / got?
    ....

4   got / she / has / a sister?
    ....

5   the family / has / any / got / pets?
    ....

6   got / she / has / a mobile phone?
    ....

7   has / a TV in her bedroom / got / she?
    ....

8   got / her house / has / a garden?
    ....

Talking about the present

2   Complete the sentences using the present continuous or the present simple of the verb.

1   At the moment Julia _is listening_ to music. (listen)

2   Every day I .... at 7 o'clock. (get up)

3   What .... your friends .... now? (do)

4   What films .... she ....? (like)

5   We .... in a big house in Cambridge. (live)

6   Where .... your dad ....? (work)

7   They .... computer games right now. (play)

8   What time .... you ....? (go to bed)

Talking about skills and abilities

3   Write true sentences. Use *can* or *can't*.

1   I _can't play the guitar_.

2   I ....

3   My best friend ....

4   I ....

5   My parents ....

6   I ....

Talking about rules

4 Look at the poster and match the pictures with the rules for the library.

You mustn't chew gum. ☐4

You must be quiet. ☐

You mustn't use your mobile phone. ☐

You must use your library card. ☐

You mustn't bring food or drink to the library. ☐

You must only have 6 books. ☐

You mustn't run. ☐

You mustn't drop litter. ☐

LIBRARY RULES

6 only

Communication

1 Look at Jodie's calendar and write true (*T*) or false (*F*).

1 On Wednesday Jodie's going swimming. _T_
2 On Sunday she's going to the skatepark with Polly. ......
3 On Friday she's going to Polly's house. ......
4 On Monday she's visiting her parents. ......
5 On Tuesday she's playing tennis. ......

2 🔘 **56** Listen and fill in the gap in Jodie's calendar.

3 🔘 **56** Listen again and complete the conversation.

SEPTEMBER		
Sunday 21	Monday 22	Tuesday 23
go to skatepark with Mark	visit my grandparents	go to the dentist
Wednesday 24	Thursday 25	Friday 26
go swimming		go to Polly's house

Pippa Hello?
Jodie Hi Pippa, it's Jodie. Let's go to the cinema on Thursday.
Pippa I'm ¹................... . I'm playing tennis on Thursday.
Jodie That's ²................... . What time are you playing tennis?
Pippa Um, at four o'clock.
Jodie ³................... to the cinema at ⁴................... o'clock?
Pippa That ⁵................... !
Jodie Cool. See you on Thursday!

Reading

1 **Read the text and decide if the sentences are true (*T*) or false (*F*).**

1 The ancient Greeks were in Greece 10,000 years ago. ...F....
2 The ancient Greeks had one king. ....
3 Lots of Greek families had slaves. ....
4 Some slaves worked as teachers to the children. ....
5 School was only for girls. ....
6 Greek meals were often meat, pasta and salad. ....
7 Dance was important to the ancient Greeks. ....
8 There were lots of different Greek dances. ....

Ancient Greeks

The ancient Greeks lived nearly 4,000 years ago. They loved music, drama, sport, science, art and talking! They started the Olympic Games and the first theatre.

In ancient Greece there wasn't one king or queen. Everyone lived in different city-states, such as Athens or Corinth. Men worked for the city-states and women stayed at home.

There were slaves in many Greek families. The slaves cooked, cleaned and worked in the fields. Sometimes they were teachers to the children in the family.

School was for boys, but not girls. Girls stayed at home with their mothers. In Greek houses there was a courtyard outside where families liked to listen to stories and eat meals. Meals were often fish, cheese, olives, bread and fruit. The Greeks liked wine!

Dance was very important to the ancient Greeks. Some dances were for men and some were for women. There were more than 200 ancient Greek dances! These were for sport, weddings and other celebrations.

2 **Tick the food that ancient Greeks liked.**

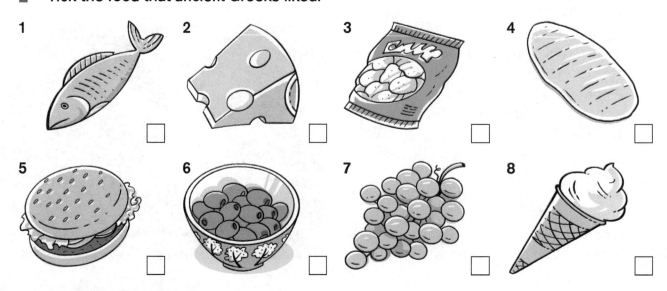

Listening

3 🔘 **57** **Listen to the voicemail messages and fill in the gaps.**

1 Hi Molly! It's Charlie. What are you **¹** _doing_ on Saturday? I'm **²** .... to the cinema with Jo and Max. Do you want to come? We're **³** .... at 3 pm. Speak to you soon!

2 Hi Charlie, Molly here! Thanks for your message. I'm **⁴** .... my grandparents on Saturday. What are you **⁵** .... on Sunday? I'm **⁶** .... pasta for my family at 1 pm. Do you want to come? Bye!

3 Hi Molly, Charlie again! I love pasta but on Sunday I'm **⁷** .... football. In the evening I'm **⁸** .... a DVD at home. Do you want to come to my house?

4 Hi Charlie! Sorry, I'm **⁹** .... my homework on Sunday evening. Oh well. See you at school on Monday!

Writing

4 **Write an email to a friend about your plans for this evening. Use these verbs to help you.**

> cook a meal   tidy your room   watch TV
> do your homework   play computer games
> do judo   go swimming   go to the shops

To:

From:

Your progress

Look at Student's Book Unit 10. Circle: ☹ **= not very well** ☺ **= quite well** 😎 **= very well**

I can write about plans for the weekend.	☹ ☺ 😎 p109
I can ask and answer questions about future arrangements.	☹ ☺ 😎 p111
I can ask and answer quiz questions using a range of language.	☹ ☺ 😎 p112
I can read and understand an article about mysteries.	☹ ☺ 😎 p116
I can listen and understand people describing where they are.	☹ ☺ 😎 p117
I can write a paragraph about a chosen topic.	☹ ☺ 😎 p117
I can make arrangements to do things with friends.	☹ ☺ 😎 p127

Your project: a class quiz

- Look on the internet for five interesting facts.
- Write five quiz questions. Remember to make a note of the correct answers!
- Write three answers for each question (a, b, and c). One answer must be correct.
- Use your questions to make a big class quiz. Give your questions to the teacher with the answers.
- Form teams and do the quiz. Your teacher asks the questions.

> Where was Elvis Presley from?
> **a)** the UK   **b)** the USA
> **c)** Canada

Grammar reference

be – positive, negative, questions and short answers

Unit 1

Positive		Negative		Questions		Short answers	
full form	short form	full form	short form				
I am	I'm	I am not	I'm not	Am	I ...?	Yes, I am.	No, I'm not.
you are	you're	you are not	you aren't	Are	you ...?	Yes, you are.	No, you aren't.
he she is it	he's she's it's	he she is not it	he she isn't it	Is	he ...? she ...? it ...?	Yes, he Yes, she is. Yes, it	No, he No, she isn't. No, it
we you are they	we're you're they're	we you are not they	we you aren't they	Are	we ...? you ...? they ...?	Yes, we Yes, you are. Yes, they	No, we No, you aren't. No, they

We use **be** to talk about name, age, nationality, colour, etc:

*I'm Jake. We **aren't** from Poland. He **isn't** French. **Are** you 13? Yes, I **am**.*

Regular plurals

Unit 1

Add **-s** to regular singular nouns to make them plural: *chair* ⟶ *chairs*

Add **-es** to nouns ending in **-ch, -sh, -s, -ss, -x, -o**: *watch* ⟶ *watches, bus* ⟶ *buses*

For nouns ending in **-y** after a consonant, change the **-y** to **-ies**: *hobby* ⟶ *hobbies*

For nouns ending in **-y** after a vowel, just add **-s**: *toy* ⟶ *toys*

Possessive adjectives

Units 1 and 2

Subject	I	you	he	she	it	we	you	they
Possessive adjective	my	your	his	her	its	our	your	their

We use a possessive adjective to say that a person or thing belongs to another.

The possessive adjective goes before the noun:

*I'm English. **My** dad is Polish. **They** are 10. **Their** sister is 12. **It** is my dog. **Its** name is Fifi.*

Question words and be

Unit 2

Question word	am / is / are	Subject
Where	's	my ruler?
Who	are	your best friends?
What	's	your favourite lesson?
When	's	her birthday?
How old	am	I?
How	are	they?

there is / there are

Unit 2

Positive	Negative	Questions	Short answers
there is	there isn't	Is there ...?	Yes, there is. / No, there isn't.
there are	there aren't	Are there ...?	Yes, there are. / No, there aren't.

We use **there is** with singular nouns and **there are** with plural nouns:

There is *a bag.* **There aren't** *six pens.* **Is there** *a desk? Yes,* **there is**.

this, that, these, those

Unit 2

We use **this** to talk about a person or thing near to us: *This is my favourite T-shirt.*
We use **these** to talk about people or things near to us: *These are my new trainers.*
We use **that** to talk about a person or thing far from us: *That is my TV on the desk.*
We use **those** to talk about people or things far from us: *Those are my books on the bed.*

have got – positive, negative, questions and short answers

Unit 3

Positive				Negative				Questions				Short answers					
I you	have 've			I you	have not haven't			Have	I you			I you	have.		I you	haven't.
he she it	has 's	got		he she it	has not hasn't	got		Has	he she it	got ...?	Yes,	he she it	has.	No,	he she it	hasn't.
we you they	have 've			we you they	have not haven't			Have	we you they			we you they	have.		we you they	haven't.

We use **have got** to talk about possession: *I've got an mp3 player. He's got a computer.*
We use *not* to form the negative: *We haven't got an umbrella. It hasn't got a camera.*
The word order changes in questions: **Has/Have** + subject + **got**: **Have** you **got** a dog?
We do not use *got* in short answers: *Have you got an eraser? Yes, I **have**. / No, I **haven't**.*

Possessive *'s*

Unit 3

We use the possessive **'s** to indicate possession: person + **'s** + possession: *Anne's car*
We use **'** when a noun or name ends in *s*: *the boys' book.*
If the possession belongs to two people, we use **'s** after the second name: *Jo and Brad's house*

Possessive pronouns and *Whose ...?*

Unit 3

Possessive adjective	my	your	his	her	its	our	your	their
Possessive pronoun	mine	yours	his	hers	–	ours	yours	theirs

We can use a possessive pronoun in place of possessive adjective + noun to say
who a person or thing belongs to: *It's her bike. It's **hers**.*
We use **Whose ...?** to ask about possession: **Whose** bag is this? It's **mine**.

Prepositions of time

Units 4 and 6

We use **in** with parts of the day, months and seasons: **in** the morning / **in** April / **in** the summer
We use **on** with days, dates and parts of a specific day: **on** Tuesday / **on** Friday morning / **on** 5th May
We use **at** with clock times and periods of time: **at** seven o'clock / **at** night / **at** the weekend

Grammar reference

Present simple – positive, negative, questions and short answers
Unit 4

Positive		Negative			Questions			Short answers					
I You	work.	w	do not don't		Do	I you		I you	do.		I you	don't.	
He She It	works.	He She It	does not doesn't	work.	Does	he she it	work?	Yes, he she it	does.	No,	he she it	doesn't.	
We You	work.	We You	do not don't		Do	we you		we you	do.		we you	don't.	

We use the present simple to talk about routines: I **get** up at 7 o'clock, regular activities:
They **play** tennis every week, and facts: We **live** in London.
The spelling of the verb changes in the third person singular. Add an **-s** to the verb:
He play**s** football after school.
Add **-es** to verbs ending in **-ch**, **-o**, **-sh**, **-s**, **-ss**, **-x**, **-z**: wash ⟶ wash**es**, go ⟶ go**es**
Add **-ies** to verbs ending in **-y** after a consonant: cry ⟶ cr**ies**

can – positive, negative, questions and short answers
Unit 5

Positive and negative			Questions			Short answers						
I You			Can	I you	run?	Yes,	I you	can.	No,	I you	can't.	
He She It	can can't	run.		he she it			he she it			he she it		
We You They				we you they			we you they			we you they		

We use **can** to talk about abilities. It has the same form for all persons (we do not add
-s to the third person singular) and it is followed by the verb without to:
I **can** skateboard. We **can't** do karate. **Can** you use a computer?

Adverbs of manner
Unit 5

Adverbs of manner describe how we do things. They go at the end of the sentence.
I can write poetry **quite well**. They can't play tennis **very well**.

like, love, hate + -ing
Unit 5

We usually use the **-ing** form of the verb after like, love and hate. With most verbs, we just add **-ing**:
Joe **likes** play**ing** chess. Amy **loves** do**ing** crosswords. We **hate** watch**ing** old films.
With verbs ending in **-e**, omit the **-e** and add **-ing**: write ⟶ writing
With 1-syllable verbs ending in vowel + consonant, double the consonant and add **-ing**: run ⟶ running

Imperatives
Unit 5

We use imperatives to give instructions, orders, warnings and advice.
We form the imperative with the base form of the verb without the subject: **Put** paper in this bin.
We form the negative by putting Don't before the imperative: **Don't** feed the animals.

Adverbs of frequency
Unit 6

We use adverbs of frequency to say how often we do things.

0%	1–20%	20–60%	60–80%	80–99%	100%
never	not often	sometimes	often	usually	always

The adverb usually goes between the subject and the main verb: *I **often have** lunch at school.*

In a negative sentence, the adverb goes between *don't / doesn't* and the verb: *I **don't often** watch TV.*

Question words and present simple
Unit 6

Question word	do / does	Subject	Verb	Other words
When	do	you	go	to school?
What	does	your friend	eat	for breakfast?
Where	do	they	go	on holiday?
Why	does	Amy	wear	pink jeans?

must – positive and negative
Unit 6

Positive	I / You / He / She / It / We / You / They	must	turn right.
Negative	I / You / He / She / It / We / You / They	mustn't	walk on the grass.

We use **must** to talk about rules and obligation. *Must* has the same form for all persons (we do not add -s to the third person singular) and it is followed by the verb without to: *You **must** be quiet in the library.* The negative form is **mustn't**: *You **mustn't** run in the corridor.*

Object pronouns
Unit 6

Subject pronoun	I	you	he	she	it	we	you	they
Object pronoun	me	you	him	her	it	us	you	them

We use object pronouns after the verb in place of the name of something or someone: *This is my new mobile phone. Do you like **it**? Mum often makes cakes. I usually help **her**.*

some or any, a or an
Unit 7

We use *some* and *any*, *a/an* to talk about quantity.

We use *some* with plural countable nouns and with uncountable nouns: **some** apples, **some** cheese

We use *some* in positive sentences and we use *any* in negative sentences and questions: *I've got **some** grapes. There aren't **any** crisps. Have you got **any** fruit juice?*

We use *a* or *an* with singular countable nouns: *There is **a** sandwich. Is there **an** apple?*

much / many / lots
Unit 7

We use **much**, **many** and **lots** to talk about quantity.

We use **much** with uncountable nouns in negative sentences and questions: *There isn't **much** water.*

We use **many** with countable nouns in negative sentences and questions: *There aren't **many** sweets.*

We use **lots (of)** in positive sentences with plural countable nouns and with uncountable nouns: *There are **lots of** apples. There's **lots of** fruit juice.*

We use **How much ...?** and **How many ...?** to ask about quantity: ***How much** milk is there? There isn't much. **How many** apples are there? There are **lots**.*

Grammar reference

Present continuous – positive, negative, questions and short answers

Unit 8

Positive			Negative			Questions			Short answers					
I	am 'm		I	am 'm not		Am	I			I	am.		I	am not. 'm not.
You	are 're		You	are not aren't		Are	you			you	are.		you	are not aren't.
He She It	is 's	eating.	He She It	is not isn't	eating.	Is	he she it	eating?	Yes,	he she it	is.	No,	he she it	is not. isn't
We You They	are 're		We You They	are not aren't		Are	we you they			we you they	are.		we you they	are not aren't.

We use the present continuous to talk about actions that are happening at the time of speaking. The form is **be** + verb + **-ing**: I**'m eating** lunch We **aren't swimming**. **Is Julia** dancing? Yes, she **is**.

Present simple or present continuous?

Unit 8

We use the present simple to talk about routine. We use the present continuous to talk about actions happening now:

Mary usually **rides** a bike.   Mary **is riding** a horse now.

Past simple verb be – positive, negative, questions and short answers

Unit 9

Positive		Negative		Questions		Short answers	
I	was	I	was not wasn't	Was	I ...?	Yes, I was.	No, I wasn't.
you	were	you	were not weren't	Were	you ...?	Yes, you were.	No, you weren't.
he she it	was	he she it	was not wasn't	Was	he ...? she ...? it ...?	Yes, he Yes, she was. Yes, it	No, he No, she wasn't. No, it
we you they	were	we you they	were not weren't	Were	we ...? you ...? they ...?	Yes, we Yes, you were. Yes, they	No, we No, you weren't. No, they

We use **was / were** to talk about situations in the past. We use **was** with I / he / she / it and **were** with you / we / they: I **was** tired. They **weren't** busy. **Was** it cold? No, it **wasn't**.

Past simple positive – regular verbs

Unit 9

We use the past simple to talk about finished situations or actions in the past.
We use the same form for all persons: We **climbed** the mountain. Harry **visited** a museum.
Add **-ed** to make the past simple of most verbs: cook ⟶ cook**ed**, watch ⟶ watch**ed**
Add **-d** to verbs ending in **-e**: arrive ⟶ arrive**d**, phone ⟶ phone**d**
With verbs ending in **-y** after a consonant, change **-y** to **-i** and add **-ed**: cry ⟶ cri**ed**
With 1-syllable verbs ending in vowel + consonant, double the consonant and add **-ed**: stop ⟶ stop**ped**

Present continuous for future arrangements

Unit 10

We use the present continuous to talk about definite arrangements in the future:
I**'m going** on a boat trip at 9.30. He**'s playing** football with Josh tomorrow.

(n) = noun (v) = verb
(adj.) = adjective

Welcome

age /eɪdʒ/
alphabet /ˈæl.fə.bet/
animal /ˈæn.ɪ.məl/
answer (v) /ˈɑːn.sə/
apple /ˈæp.əl/
April /ˈeɪ.prəl/
August /ˈɔː.gəst/
bag /bæg/
banana /bəˈnɑː.nə/
bin /bɪn/
birthday /ˈbɜːθ.deɪ/
black /blæk/
blue /bluː/
board /bɔːd/
book (n) /bʊk/
bookcase /ˈbʊk.keɪs/
boy /bɔɪ/
brown /braʊn/
bye /baɪ/
calculator /ˈkæl.kjə.leɪ.tə/
chair /tʃeə/
classroom /ˈklɑːs.rʊm/
clock /klɒk/
colour (n) /ˈkʌl.ə/
computer /kəmˈpjuː.tə/
conversation
    /ˌkɒn.və.ˈseɪ.ʃən/
cool /kuːl/
dad /dæd/
date /deɪt/
day /deɪ/
December /dɪˈsem.bə/
desk /desk/
diary /ˈdaɪə.ri/
English /ˈɪŋ.glɪʃ/
eraser /ɪˈreɪzə/
family /ˈfæm.əl.i/
fashion /ˈfæʃ.ən/
favourite /ˈfeɪ.vər.ɪt/
February /ˈfeb.ru.ər.i/
film (n) /fɪlm/
fine (adj) /faɪn/
Friday /ˈfraɪ.deɪ/
friend /frend/
fun /fʌn/
girl /gɜːl/
good evening
    /ˌgʊd ˈiː.vən.ɪŋ/
good morning
    /ˌgʊd ˈmɔː.nɪŋ/
good night /ˌgʊd ˈnaɪt/
goodbye /gʊdˈbaɪ/
green /griːn/
group /gruːp/

hand /hænd/
hear /hɪə/
hello /heˈləʊ/
hi /haɪ/
house /haʊs/
ice cream /ˌaɪs ˈkriːm/
interest /ˈɪn.trəst/
interview (n) /ˈɪn.tə.vjuː/
January /ˈdʒæn.ju.ər.i/
join in /ˌdʒɔɪn ˈɪn/
July /dʒʊˈlaɪ/
June /dʒuːn/
late /leɪt/
letter /ˈlet.ə/
lunchtime /ˈlʌntʃ.taɪm/
make /meɪk/
map /mæp/
March /mɑːtʃ/
May /meɪ/
Monday /ˈmʌn.deɪ/
month /mʌnθ/
moon /muːn/
Mr /ˈmɪs.tə/
Mrs /ˈmɪs.ɪz/
mum /mʌm/
music /ˈmjuː.zɪk/
name /neɪm/
next door /ˌnekst ˈdɔː/
November /nəʊˈvem.bə/
number /ˈnʌm.bə/
o'clock /əˈklɒk/
October /ɒkˈtəʊ.bə/
old /əʊld/
open (v) /ˈəʊ.pən/
orange (adj) /ˈɒr.ɪndʒ/
park (n) /pɑːk/
pen /pen/
pencil /ˈpen.səl/
pencil case /ˈpen.səl ˌkeɪs/
phone (n) /fəʊn/
photo /ˈfəʊ.təʊ/
pink /pɪŋk/
pizza /ˈpiːt.sə/
please /pliːz/
Poland /ˈpəʊ.lənd/
poster /ˈpəʊ.stə/
purple /ˈpɜː.pəl/
quarter /ˈkwɔː.tə/
question /ˈkwes.tʃən/
red /red/
ruler /ˈruː.lə/
Saturday /ˈsæt.ə.deɪ/
school /skuːl/
school bag /ˈskuːl.bæg/
September /sepˈtem.bə/
sit /sɪt/
slowly /ˈsləʊli/
song /sɒŋ/
sorry /ˈsɒr.i/
speak /spiːk/

sport /spɔːt/
stand /stænd/
story /ˈstɔː.ri/
student /ˈstjuː.dənt/
sun /sʌn/
Sunday /ˈsʌn.deɪ/
table /ˈteɪ.bəl/
teacher /ˈtiː.tʃə/
telephone /ˈtel.ɪ.fəʊn/
tell the time /ˌtel ˌðə ˈtaɪm/
thanks /θæŋks/
thing /θɪŋ/
Thursday /ˈθɜːz.deɪ/
Tuesday /ˈtʃuːz.deɪ/
UK /ˌjuːˈkeɪ/
umbrella /ʌmˈbrel.ə/
understand /ˌʌn.dəˈstænd/
warm /wɔːm/
watch (n) /wɒtʃ/
Wednesday /ˈwenz.deɪ/
week /wiːk/
weekend /ˌwiːkˈend/
white /waɪt/
window /ˈwɪn.dəʊ/
word /wɜːd/
world /wɜːld/
write /raɪt/
yellow /ˈjel.əʊ/

Unit 1

actor /ˈæk.tə/
address /əˈdres/
America /əˈmer.ɪ.kə/
American /əˈmer.ɪ.kən/
artist /ˈɑː.tɪst/
Australia /ɒsˈtreɪ.li.ə/
Australian /ɒsˈtreɪ.liən/
band /bænd/
basketball /ˈbɑː.skɪt.bɔːl/
bicycle /ˈbaɪ.sɪ.kəl/
big /bɪg/
box /bɒks/
boy /bɔɪ/
Brazil /brəˈzɪl/
Brazilian /brəˈzɪl.i.ən/
British /ˈbrɪt.ɪʃ/
brother /ˈbrʌð.ə/
café /ˈkæf.eɪ/
car /kɑː/
cat /kæt/
China /ˈtʃaɪ.nə/
Chinese /tʃaɪˈniːz/
city /ˈsɪt.i/
class /klɑːs/
club /klʌb/
country /ˈkʌn.tri/
dog /dɒg/
Earth /ɜːθ/

easy /ˈiː.zi/
England /ˈɪŋ.glənd/
fan /fæn/
favourite /ˈfeɪ.vər.ɪt/
fish (n) /fɪʃ/
football /ˈfʊt.bɔːl/
France /frɑːns/
French /frentʃ/
game /geɪm/
German /ˈdʒɜː.mən/
glasses /ˈglɑː.sɪz/
good /gʊd/
great /greɪt/
Greece /griːs/
Greek /griːk/
guitar /gɪˈtɑː/
hamster /ˈhæmp.stə/
here /hɪə/
hobby /ˈhɒb.i/
home /həʊm/
horse /hɔːs/
hurry /ˈhʌr.i/
idea /aɪˈdɪə/
India /ˈɪn.di.ə/
Indian /ˈɪn.diən/
internet /ˈɪn.tə.net/
Ireland /ˈaɪə.lənd/
Irish /ˈaɪə.rɪʃ/
jacket /ˈdʒæk.ɪt/
job /dʒɒb/
key /kiː/
lesson /ˈles.ən/
life /laɪf/
mobile (phone) /ˈməʊ.baɪl/
money /ˈmʌn.i/
museum /mjuːˈziː.əm/
nationality /ˌnæʃ.ənˈæl.ə.ti/
naughty /ˈnɔː.ti/
nice /naɪs/
parent /ˈpeə.rənt/
penpal /ˈpen.pæl/
people /ˈpiː.pəl/
player /pleɪə/
playground /ˈpleɪ.graʊnd/
Polish /ˈpəʊ.lɪʃ/
post (v) /pəʊst/
potato /pəˈteɪ.təʊ/
programme /ˈprəʊ.græm/
quickly /ˈkwɪk.li/
right /raɪt/
ringtone /ˈrɪŋ.təʊn/
room /ruːm/
sandwich /ˈsæn.wɪdʒ/
scarf /skɑːf/
science /ˈsaɪ.əns/
Scotland /ˈskɒt.lənd/
see /siː/
sentence /ˈsen.təns/
shirt /ʃɜːt/
silly /ˈsɪl.i/

singer /'sɪŋ.ə/
sister /'sɪs.tə/
small /smɔːl/
Spain /speɪn/
Spanish /'spæn.ɪʃ/
study (v) /'stʌd.i/
Sweden /'swiː.dən/
Swedish /'swiː.dɪʃ/
swim /swɪm/
team /tiːm/
tennis /'ten.ɪs/
think /θɪŋk/
tomato /tə'mɑː.təʊ/
too /tuː/
town /taʊn/
toy /tɔɪ/
t-shirt /'tiː.ʃɜːt/
Turkey /'tɜː.ki/
TV /ˌtiː'viː/
wrong /rɒŋ/
year /jɪə/
yes /jes/

Unit 2

amazing /ə'meɪ.zɪŋ/
apartment /ə'pɑːt.mənt/
armchair /'ɑːm.tʃeə/
bathroom /'bɑːθ.rʊm/
bed /bed/
bedroom /'bed.rʊm/
bird /bɜːd/
black /blæk/
boat /bəʊt/
breakfast /'brek.fəst/
brilliant /'brɪl.i.ənt/
bus /bʌs/
busy /'bɪz.i/
castle /'kɑː.səl/
cave /keɪv/
child /tʃaɪld/
children /'tʃɪl.drən/
cinema /'sɪn.ə.mə/
come /kʌm/
cornflakes /'kɔːn.fleɪks/
cosy /'kəʊ.zi/
curtain /'kɜː.tən/
cushion /'kʊʃ.ən/
dear /dɪə/
dining room /'daɪn.ɪŋ ˌruːm/
doctor /'dɒk.tə/
door /dɔː/
dream (adj) /driːm/
end (n) /end/
expensive /ɪk'spen.sɪv/
fantastic /fæn'tæs.tɪk/
feet /fiːt/
food /fuːd/
foot /fʊt/
footballer /'fʊt.bɔː.lə/
forest /'fɒr.ɪst/

funny /'fʌn.i/
garage /'gær.ɑːʒ/
garden /'gɑː.dən/
go /gəʊ/
gym /dʒɪm/
hall /hɔːl/
happy /'hæp.i/
have got /hæv 'gɒt/
holiday /'hɒl.ə.deɪ/
horrible /'hɒr.ə.bəl/
houseboat /'haʊs.bəʊt/
in front of /ɪn 'frʌnt ɒv/
kitchen /'kɪtʃ.ɪn/
know /nəʊ/
lake /leɪk/
lamp /læmp/
library /'laɪ.brər.i/
living room /'lɪv.ɪŋ ˌrʊm/
long /lɒŋ/
look /lʊk/
lots of /'lɒts ɒv/
love (v) /lʌv/
lunch /lʌntʃ/
market /'mɑː.kɪt/
mess /mes/
Mexico /'mek.sɪ.kəʊ/
Morocco /mə'rɒk.əʊ/
night /naɪt/
now /naʊ/
only /'əʊn.li/
other /'ʌð.ə/
palace /'pæl.ɪs/
penfriend /'pen.frend/
perfect /'pɜː.fɪkt/
person /'pɜː.sən/
quiet /'kwaɪət/
restaurant /'res.tər.ɒnt/
river /'rɪv.ə/
rug /rʌg/
sea /siː/
serious /'sɪə.ri.əs/
sofa /'səʊ.fə/
strange /streɪndʒ/
stuff /stʌf/
swimming pool
    /'swɪmɪŋ ˌpuːl/
teenager /'tiː.neɪ.dʒə/
tennis court /'ten.ɪs ˌkɔːt/
today /tə'deɪ/
toilet /'tɔɪ.lət/
trainers /'treɪn.əz/
tree /triː/
trip /trɪp/
Wales /weɪlz/
walk (v) /wɔːk/
wall /wɔːl/
wardrobe /'wɔː.drəʊb/
well /wel/
wooden /'wʊd.ən/

Unit 3

aunt /ɑːnt/
Auntie /'ɑːn.ti/
bike /baɪk/
boyfriend /'bɔɪ.frend/
camera /'kæm.rə/
clever /'klev.ə/
cousin /'kʌz.ən/
curly /'kɜː.li/
dark /dɑːk/
daughter /'dɔː.tə/
difficult /'dɪf.ɪ.kəlt/
eye /aɪ/
fair /feə/
friendly /'frend.li/
frog /frɒg/
gran /græn/
grandad /'græn.dæd/
grandfather /'grænd.fɑː.ðə/
grandmother
    /'grænd.mʌð.ə/
grandparent
    /'grænd.peə.rənt/
hair /heə/
hat /hæt/
homework /'həʊm.wɜːk/
husband /'hʌz.bənd/
joke /dʒəʊk/
kind /kaɪnd/
lizard /'lɪz.əd/
memory /'mem.ər.i/
mother /'mʌð.ə/
mp3 player
    /ˌem.piː'θriː pleɪə/
OK /əʊ'keɪ/
parrot /'pær.ət/
plump /plʌmp/
shy /ʃaɪ/
skateboard /'skeɪt.bɔːd/
slim /slɪm/
son /sʌn/
spider /'spaɪ.də/
stepfather /'step.fɑː.ðə/
stepmother /'step.mʌð.ə/
straight /streɪt/
tall /tɔːl/
tortoise /'tɔː.təs/
uncle /'ʌŋ.kəl/
wife /waɪf/

Unit 4

blog /blɒg/
boring /'bɔː.rɪŋ/
buy /baɪ/
cake /keɪk/
circus /'sɜː.kəs/
clean (v) /kliːn/
clothes /kləʊðz/
coffee /'kɒf.i/

collect /kə'lekt/
Colombia /kə'lɒm.bi.ə/
cry /kraɪ/
dance (v) /dɑːns/
dinner /'dɪn.ə/
drink (v) /drɪŋk/
drive /draɪv/
driver /'draɪ.və/
eat /iːt/
exciting /ɪk'saɪ.tɪŋ/
famous /'feɪ.məs/
farmer /'fɑː.mə/
finish /'fɪn.ɪʃ/
get dressed /ˌget 'drest/
go shopping /ˌgəʊ 'ʃɒpɪŋ/
go to sleep /ˌgəʊ tə'sliːp/
guess /ges/
hairdresser /'heə.dres.ə/
hate /heɪt/
high wire /'haɪ.waɪə/
hour /aʊə/
instrument /'ɪnt.strə.mənt/
jam /dʒæm/
Japan /dʒə'pæn/
like /laɪk/
live (v) /lɪv/
meal /miːl/
mechanic /mɪ'kæn.ɪk/
meet /miːt/
musical /'mjuː.zɪ.kəl/
newspaper /'njuːs.peɪ.pə/
office /'ɒf.ɪs/
outside /ˌaʊt'saɪd/
party /'pɑː.ti/
performer /pə'fɔː.mə/
play (v) /pleɪ/
police officer
    /pə'liːs ˌɒf.ɪ.sə/
practice /'præk.tɪs/
prepare /prɪ'peə/
questionnaire
    /ˌkwes.tʃə'neə/
record (n) /'rek.ɔːd/
shop /ʃɒp/
shop assistant
    /'ʃɒp ə.sɪs.tənt/
shower /'ʃaʊ.ə/
sing /sɪŋ/
skin /skɪn/
sleep /sliːp/
special /'speʃ.əl/
spend /spend/
start /stɑːt/
take /teɪk/
tea /tiː/
terrible /'ter.ə.bəl/
test (v) /test/
text message
    /'tekst ˌmes.ɪdʒ/
the Web /ðə 'web/
tired /taɪəd/

toast /təʊst/
together /təˈgeð.ə/
trapeze /trəˈpiːz/
travel /ˈtræv.əl/
uniform /ˈjuː.nɪ.fɔːm/
wake up /ˌweɪk ˈʌp/
watch (v) /wɒtʃ/
way /weɪ/
wear /weə/
worker /ˈwɜː.kə/
zoo keeper /ˈzuːˌkiː.pə/

Unit 5

ball /bɔːl/
competition /ˌkɒm.pəˈtɪʃ.ən/
crossword /ˈkrɒs.wɜːd/
cycle /ˈsaɪ.kəl/
disco /ˈdɪs.kəʊ/
elephant /ˈel.ɪ.fənt/
feed /fiːd/
get up /get ˈʌp/
gorilla /gəˈrɪl.ə/
gymnastics /dʒɪmˈnæs.tɪks/
handstand /ˈhænd.stænd/
hey /heɪ/
hippo /ˈhɪp.əʊ/
juggle /ˈdʒʌg.əl/
karate /kəˈrɑː.ti/
keep fit /ˌkiːp ˈfɪt/
learn /lɜːn/
leg /leg/
many /ˈmen.i/
maths /mæθs/
minute /ˈmɪnɪt/
mostly /ˈməʊst.li/
noise /nɔɪz/
of course /ɒv ˈkɔːs/
ostrich /ˈɒs.trɪtʃ/
paint /peɪnt/
piano /ˈpjæ.nəʊ/
picnic /ˈpɪk.nɪk/
poetry /ˈpəʊ.ə.tri/
puzzle /ˈpʌz.əl/
quite /kwaɪt/
race /reɪs/
rest (v) /rest/
ride (v) /raɪd/
rock music /ˈrɒk ˌmjuː.zɪk/
row /rəʊ/
rugby /ˈrʌg.bi/
run /rʌn/
secret /ˈsiː.krət/
skate /skeɪt/
ski /skiː/
snail /sneɪl/
snake /sneɪk/
summer /ˈsʌm.ə/
take photos /teɪk ˈfəʊ.təʊz/
test (n) /test/
useful /ˈjuːs.fəl/

volleyball /ˈvɒl.i.bɔːl/
want /wɒnt/
weird /wɪəd/
well /wel/
whale /weɪl/
win /wɪn/

Unit 6

always /ˈɔːl.weɪz/
believe /bɪˈliːv/
body /ˈbɒd.i/
break (n) /breɪk/
bring /brɪŋ/
canteen /kænˈtiːn/
coat /kəʊt/
concert /ˈkɒn.sɜːt/
corridor /ˈkɒr.ɪ.dɔː/
creative /kriˈeɪ.tɪv/
drama /ˈdrɑː.mə/
dress (n) /dres/
drop /drɒp/
enjoy /ɪnˈdʒɔɪ/
experiment /ɪkˈsper.ɪ.mənt/
fruit /fruːt/
geography /dʒiˈɒg.rə.fi/
German /ˈdʒɜː.mən/
grass /grɑːs/
history /ˈhɪs.tər.i/
ICT /ˌaɪ.siːˈtiː/
jazz dance /ˈdʒæz ˌdɑːns/
later /ˈleɪt.ə/
litter /ˈlɪt.ə/
mask /mɑːsk/
meat /miːt/
Miss /mɪs/
move /muːv/
musician /mjuːˈzɪʃ.ən/
never /ˈnev.ə/
often /ˈɒf.ən/
orchestra /ˈɔː.kɪ.strə/
pasta /ˈpæs.tə/
PE /ˌpiːˈiː/
piece /piːs/
polite /pəˈlaɪt/
prefer /prɪˈfɜː/
primary school
　/ˈpraɪ.mər.i ˌskuːl/
project /ˈprɒ.dʒekt/
religious education
　/rɪˈlɪdʒ.əs ˌedʒ.ʊˈkeɪ.ʃən/
remember /rɪˈmem.bə/
secondary school
　/ˈsek.ən.dər.i skuːl/
shoe /ʃuː/
skirt /skɜːt/
sometimes /ˈsʌm.taɪmz/
studio /ˈstjuː.di.əʊ/
supermarket
　/ˈsuː.pəˌmɑː.kɪt/
sure /ʃɔː/

sweater /ˈswet.ə/
sweatshirt /ˈswet.ʃɜːt/
sweet /swiːt/
thank you /ˈθæŋk.juː/
tie (n) /taɪ/
timetable /ˈtaɪmˌteɪ.bəl/
trousers /ˈtraʊ.zəz/
turn /tɜːn/
usually /ˈjuː.ʒəli/
vegetarian /ˌvedʒ.ɪˈteə.ri.ən/

Unit 7

ago /əˈgəʊ/
bean /biːn/
beef /biːf/
biscuit /ˈbɪs.kɪt/
blonde /blɒnd/
bottle /ˈbɒt.əl/
bread /bred/
building /ˈbɪld.ɪŋ/
burger /ˈbɜː.gə/
card /kɑːd/
carrot /ˈkær.ət/
cheese /tʃiːz/
chicken /ˈtʃɪk.ɪn/
chip /tʃɪp/
cola /ˈkəʊ.lə/
comic /ˈkɒm.ɪk/
crisp /krɪsp/
curry /ˈkʌr.i/
dessert /dɪˈzɜːt/
diet /daɪət/
egg /eg/
fly (v) /flaɪ/
freezer /ˈfriː.zə/
fridge /frɪdʒ/
grape /greɪp/
ham /hæm/
hamburger /ˈhæmˌbɜː.gə/
healthy /ˈhel.θi/
hurray /həˈreɪ/
juice /dʒuːs/
junk food /ˈdʒʌŋk ˌfuːd/
lamb /læm/
lemonade /ˌlem.əˈneɪd/
little /ˈlɪt.əl/
luggage /ˈlʌg.ɪdʒ/
melon /ˈmel.ən/
menu /ˈmen.juː/
milk /mɪlk/
nut /nʌt/
orange (n) /ˈɒr.ɪndʒ/
packed lunch /ˌpækt ˈlʌntʃ/
pea /piː/
pear /peə/
pie /paɪ/
problem /ˈprɒb.ləm/
rain (n) /reɪn/
religion /rɪˈlɪdʒ.ən/
salad /ˈsæl.əd/

serve /sɜːv/
snack /snæk/
soup /suːp/
spinach /ˈspɪn.ɪtʃ/
strawberry /ˈstrɔː.bər.i/
strong /strɒŋ/
sugar /ˈʃʊg.ə/
tonight /təˈnaɪt/
tray /treɪ/
trolley /ˈtrɒl.i/
vegetable /ˈvedʒ.tə.bəl/
wait /weɪt/
website /ˈweb.saɪt/
yoghurt /ˈjɒg.ət/

Unit 8

angry /ˈæŋ.gri/
bat /bæt/
bear /beə/
big wheel /ˌbɪg ˈwiːl/
bored /bɔːd/
call /kɔːl/
cathedral /kəˈθiː.drəl/
classmate /ˈklɑːs.meɪt/
cloudy /ˈklaʊ.di/
excited /ɪkˈsaɪ.tɪd/
fall /fɔːl/
fast /fɑːst/
feel /fiːl/
feeling /ˈfiː.lɪŋ/
ferry /ˈfer.i/
fight /faɪt/
foggy /ˈfɒg.i/
gift /gɪft/
giraffe /dʒɪˈrɑːf/
hill /hɪl/
hungry /ˈhʌŋ.gri/
insect /ˈɪn.sekt/
interested /ˈɪn.trəstɪd/
jeans /dʒiːnz/
kangaroo /ˌkæŋ.gərˈuː/
keep a diary
　/kiːp ə ˈdaɪə.ri/
knight /naɪt/
koala /kəʊˈɑː.lə/
look /lʊk/
lose /luːz/
model /ˈmɒd.əl/
north-west /ˌnɔːθˈwest/
port /pɔːt/
prize /praɪz/
rain (v) /reɪn/
ride (n) /raɪd/
sad /sæd/
scared /skeəd/
ship /ʃɪp/
snow (v) /snəʊ/
south /saʊθ/
stop /stɒp/
street /striːt/

sunny /ˈsʌn.i/
theme park /ˈθiːm ˌpɑːk/
thirsty /ˈθɜː.sti/
tiger /ˈtaɪ.gə/
tour /tʊə/
violin /ˌvaɪ.əˈlɪn/
windy /ˈwɪn.di/

Unit 9

adventure /ˌədˈven.tʃə/
Africa /ˈæf.rɪ.kə/
agree /əˈɡriː/
already /ˌɔːlˈred.i/
Asia /ˈeɪ.ʒə/
astronaut /ˈæs.trə.nɔːt/
baby /ˈbeɪ.bi/
beautiful /ˈbjuː.tɪ.fəl/
born /bɔːn/
camel /ˈkæm.əl/
carpet /ˈkɑː.pɪt/
carry /ˈkær.i/
cheap /tʃiːp/
cost /kɒst/
dangerous /ˈdeɪn.dʒər.əs/
decide /dɪˈsaɪd/
desert /ˈdez.ət/
dinosaur /ˈdaɪ.nə.sɔː/
drum /drʌm/
exhibition /ˌek.sɪˈbɪʃ.ən/
explorer /ˌɪkˈsplɔː.rə/
fancy dress /ˌfæn.si ˈdres/
finally /ˈfaɪ.nəli/
first /ˈfɜːst/
follow /ˈfɒl.əʊ/
helicopter /ˈhel.ɪ.kɒp.tə/

invention /ɪnˈven.ʃən/
Italy /ˈɪt.əl.i/
journey /ˈdʒɜː.ni/
kilometre /ˌkɪˈlɒm.ɪ.tə/
land (n) /lænd/
last (v) /lɑːst/
leader /ˈliː.də/
machine /məˈʃiːn/
marry /ˈmær.i/
mean (v) /miːn/
metre /ˈmiː.tə/
miss (v) /mɪs/
motorbike /ˈməʊ.tə.baɪk/
news /njuːz/
noisy /ˈnɔɪ.zi/
ocean /ˈəʊ.ʃən/
offer (v) /ˈɒf.ə/
orbit (v) /ˈɔː.bɪt/
panda /ˈpæn.də/
parachute /ˈpær.ə.ʃuːt/
plane /pleɪn/
poor /pɔː/
relaxed /rɪˈlækst/
return /rɪˈtɜːn/
rich /rɪtʃ/
Russia /ˈrʌʃ.ə/
safe /seɪf/
sail (v) /seɪl/
satnav /ˈsæt.næv/
skeleton /ˈskel.ɪ.tən/
step (n) /step/
storm /stɔːm/
storyteller /ˈstɔː.ri.tel.ə/
surprise /səˈpraɪz/
toothbrush /ˈtuːθ.brʌʃ/
top /tɒp/

touch /tʌtʃ/
train /treɪn/
transport /ˈtræn.spɔːt/
traveller /ˈtræv.əl.ə/
ugly /ˈʌɡ.li/
view /vjuː/
wonderful /ˈwʌn.də.fəl/
yacht /jɒt/
yesterday /ˈjes.tə.deɪ/
youth club /ˈjuːθ ˌklʌb/

Unit 10

airport /ˈeə.pɔːt/
alien /ˈeɪ.li.ən/
ancient /ˈeɪn.ʃənt/
ape /eɪp/
author /ˈɔː.θə/
begin /bɪˈɡɪn/
button /ˈbʌt.ən/
disagree /ˌdɪs.əˈɡriː/
disappear /ˌdɪs.əˈpɪə/
Egypt /ˈiː.dʒɪpt/
Egyptian /iˈdʒɪp.ʃən/
flag /flæɡ/
footprint /ˈfʊt.prɪnt/
giant /dʒaɪ.ənt/
goldfish /ˈɡəʊld.fɪʃ/
happen /ˈhæp.ən/
hotel /həʊˈtel/
human /ˈhjuː.mən/
island /ˈaɪ.lənd/
leave /liːv/
light (n) /laɪt/
lion /laɪ.ən/
litre /ˈliː.tə/

lost /lɒst/
moment /ˈməʊ.mənt/
monster /ˈmɒn.stə/
mystery /ˈmɪs.tər.i/
neck /nek/
novel /ˈnɒv.əl/
object /ˈɒb.dʒekt/
painting /ˈpeɪn.tɪŋ/
philosopher /fɪˈlɒs.ə.fə/
photograph /ˈfəʊ.tə.ɡrɑːf/
photographer /fəˈtɒɡ.rə.fə/
plan (n) /plæn/
planet /ˈplæn.ɪt/
press (v) /pres/
quiz /kwɪz/
rainforest /ˈreɪnˌfɒr.ɪst/
Roman /ˈrəʊ.mən/
Russian /ˈrʌʃ.ən/
save /seɪv/
scary /ˈskeə.ri/
scientist /ˈsaɪ.ən.tɪst/
second (n) /ˈsek.ənd/
similar /ˈsɪm.ɪ.lə/
sky /skaɪ/
sound (v) /saʊnd/
star /stɑː/
station /ˈsteɪ.ʃən/
still /stɪl/
sure /ʃɔː/
surprising /səˈpraɪ.zɪŋ/
then /ðen/
tidy (v) /ˈtaɪ.di/
tomorrow /ˌtəˈmɒr.əʊ/
turn off /ˌtɜːn ˈɒf/
turn on /ˌtɜːn ˈɒn/
UFO /ˌjuː.efˈəʊ/

Phonetic symbols

Consonants

/p/	pen	/m/	make	/j/	you
/b/	be	/n/	nice	/h/	he
/t/	two	/ŋ/	sing	/θ/	thing
/d/	do	/s/	see	/ð/	this
/k/	can	/z/	trousers	/ʃ/	she
/ɡ/	good	/w/	we	/tʃ/	cheese
/f/	five	/l/	listen	/ʒ/	usually
/v/	very	/r/	right	/dʒ/	German

Vowels

/æ/	man	/iː/	see
/ɑː/	father	/ʊ/	book
/e/	ten	/uː/	food
/ɜː/	thirteen	/ʌ/	up
/ə/	mother	/ɒ/	hot
/ɪ/	sit	/ɔː/	four

Diphthongs

/eɪ/	great	/eə/	chair
/aɪ/	fine	/aʊ/	town
/ɔɪ/	boy	/əʊ/	go
/ɪə/	hear	/ʊə/	pure